WHEN DEATH COMES

A BIBLICAL STUDY OF DEATH AND THE AFTERLIFE

All Scripture quotations in this book are taken from the King James translation of the Bible.

When Death Comes
Copyright © 2004 by Keith Harris
P.O. Box 1353 Madisonville, KY 42431
www.scripture2scripture.com
Published by The Olive Press
An Olive Press Production

Copy Typist:	Keith Harris
Copy Editor:	Susanna Cancassi
Proofreaders:	Angie Peters and Susanna Cancassi
Layout/Design:	Michelle Kim
Lithography:	Simon Froese
Cover Design:	Michelle Kim

Library of Congress Cataloging-in-Publication Data

Harris, Keith
    When Death Comes
    ISBN# 0-937422-59-2

    1. Prophecy

Printed in the United States of America

This book
is dedicated to
Dad and Mom,
Loyd and Melva Harris,
who taught me much about love, life,
and
Jesus Christ.

CONTENTS

Chapter 7   131

SUICIDE

• Out Of What? • King Saul • Saul's Servant • Zimri •
Ahithophel • Abimelech And Assisted Suicide • Judas Iscariot
• Problem Source • Judas' Reflection • Judas' Suicide •
Suicide Reflection • Son Of Perdition • His Own Place •
Godly Subjection • Hope And Help

Chapter 8   163

THE DEATH OF A CHILD

• For Of Such Is The Kingdom Of God • Child Salvation •
Age Of Accountability • He Took A Child • Blaming God •
Abortion • God's Gift • Playing God • Abortion Biblical? •
Life Begins At Conception • Forgiveness • Perspective

Chapter 9   181

CONCERNING LAST THINGS:
CREMATION OR BURIAL

• Ashes To Ashes, Dust To Dust • Cremation • Fire Offering •
Modern Cremation • Biblical Cremation • The Burning Of Saul
• God's Cremation • Biblical Burial • Graves Opened

8

INTRODUCTION

Death is not a period, but a comma
in the story of life.

Losing a loved one to death is difficult and sometimes hard to understand. Many times we find ourselves asking why. During those times we need answers, not only when questions about mortality concern our loved ones, but also when they concern us as well.

More often than not, the reality of death doesn't hit home until doctors have done all they can do, and we're left to try and postpone the inevitable. It may be the unexpected passing of a loved one, or a terrorist attack against the masses; it may even be a personal brush with death that sounds the wake-up call. Whatever the situation may be, as quickly as the call rings out, we see the reality of life; we see death.

Every city, village and community bears testimony to this dreaded enemy. Cemeteries, headstones, obituaries and memorials cry out that death is present and it is very real. Every individual is summoned by death's call and inches his way toward meeting this foe. But the story doesn't end there: There is more to life than dying and more to death than becoming non-existent. Death is only a comma in the story of life.

Contrary to common belief, death is not a gloom and doom subject. It is a subject that we can understand, and one by which we may be inspired. Writing under the inspiration of the Holy Spirit, the Apostle Paul revealed great confidence concerning death and dying. His writings reflect that death is gain for those who are properly prepared for it (Phil. 1:20–24). If it is gain, then it is not loss. Therefore, all we need is proper perspective and preparation, which will widen our vision, dispel confusion, vanquish fear and usher in a satisfying hope.

Religion and Death

If you have ever been called upon to counsel the aged, the terminally ill, or those who are just beginning to question the mysteries of life and death, you will realize that mere human perspective is not enough to satisfy the mind. Personal opinion, near-death experiences, out-of-body phenomena, or fantastic dream-world ideas cannot supply the proper and satisfactory answers to our questions.

Even religion cannot supply adequate answers when death comes. In fact, religion is very deceptive in and of itself. It is a far cry from what Creator God intended. For instance, the ancient Egyptians were very religious, but their beliefs were based upon pagan myth and allegory descending from the mystery religions of ancient Babylon, not upon the Creator's plan for mankind.

The Old Testament followers of the one true God were warned against following the Egyptian religion (Ezek. 20:7). Such worship often led God's people astray. As a result, ancient Egypt perished (Ezek. 29:8–12). The remains of the ancient people continue to be dispersed among the countries of the world and are desolate (*shemamah* in the Hebrew); that is, their devastation continues to be an astonishment. Shortly after the dispersion of the empire, a remnant returned to Egypt, but this was only a menial existence in light of their former glory (Ezek. 29:11).

The ancient Egyptians preserved their dead by mummification and supplied their deceased with goods for the next life. Moses, who was learned in all the wisdom of the Egyptians (Acts 7:22), was not instructed by God to include their practices when penning the first five books of the Old Testament. Why? Because these beliefs were based upon a false hope fostered by ideas opposed to God's plan.

For example, Hinduism teaches that death is only an avenue to a better status in life through the transmigration of the soul, or reincarnation, as it is more commonly known. They believe that if a person has behaved well in this life, he will return to a better life experience. If one has behaved badly in this life, they believe that he will be reborn and suffer greatly for his past sins. This thought, as well as that of the ancient Egyptians, is in no way related to the message from God. Such theories may be fanciful and comfortable to live by but they are built upon pagan myth and speculation. They are certainly not good to die by. We cannot trust mere religion.

Fantasy

A popular fantasy shared by many people is that

they will eventually enter a place or state of heavenly bliss regardless of their lifestyle choices. This scenario depicts deceased loved ones peering down from heaven with big grins on their faces as if to say, "Just wait until you get here; it's wonderful." Heaven *is* truly wonderful, but we cannot trust fantasy.

We should know that our lives are only a span of time set aside so that we may make preparations to meet death and everything that follows. This time is made up of choices; subsequently, the choices we make greatly affect our method of departure and determine our experiences beyond death. If we are honest with ourselves, we will realize that we need more than deceptive religion or personal whim in order to make intelligent choices.

There is but one place to find wise and proper answers: Creator God. We must trust what God has established as truth and look beyond what is considered relative. That is why this book is based on the Bible. It is there that we find assurance in life and in death. Personal opinions don't count—not mine and not yours. If we want the truth, we must study God's Word and accept its revelation: either God is correct or He is not.

We will delve into God's Word in the following pages to find the much sought-after answers concerning death and what is often termed as the "afterlife." We will also discuss the proper steps to prepare for the coming transformation of death. This study is not based on fantasy or story-telling, it is simply a study based upon God's Word.

In the most loving and caring attitude, I pray this study will encourage each person to experience a fearless approach to death. Ω

CHAPTER
1

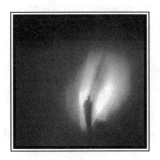

OUR COMMON ENEMY

On her deathbed, Queen Elizabeth of
England cried out to her maids of honor, "Can
you not drive off death? I will give all my possessions for a moment more of time."

Rich or poor, bond or free, every person falls prey to death. Like God, death is no respecter of persons. Whether you are a king or a pauper, you are not exempt. Every strategy of escape will become of little value when death knocks on your door. When death comes, medical discoveries, disciplines or inventions will be of no consequence.

Death is so well established that neither wealth nor power can dissuade it. It cannot be bought, bribed or defeated. You can't out-run it or out-smart it. Even love must step aside for death. You may choose to ignore it or even deny it, but when death calls, you must answer.

As a result of Adam's sin, death was made the common lot of all people, therefore it is our common enemy. The Apostle Paul wrote that death is the last enemy to be destroyed (I Cor. 15:26). This means that death will be around for a long time. Therefore, it would be wise, in a preparatory sense, to get to know the enemy.

Like a military strategist, we must know our enemy and prepare for a victory. If we know what to expect and how to properly prepare for the appointed confrontation, we need not fear the dreaded enemy called death.

The Appointment of Death

Hebrews 9:27 says that it is appointed unto men once to die. This poses a question: Is a specific year, month, day, hour, minute or second scheduled for our time of death?

The word "appointed" comes from the Greek word *apokeimai,* meaning "to be reserved; figuratively, to await: laid up." This tells us that death has been reserved for man. It does not necessarily mean that a specific date or time has been set for each of us to die. It simply means that a reservation for our death has been made. Although dates or times for reservations are usually made in advance, reservations may be changed.

Many individuals have had their reservations rescheduled. For instance, Hezekiah prayed and fifteen years were added to his life (II Kings 20:1–6). This still happens today through intercessory prayer and God's intervention. Enoch walked with God and had his reservation completely cancelled because God took him (Gen. 5:24; Heb. 11:5).

These examples relate that a time or date for one's death is not set in concrete, but that it is reserved for each individual. Many variables make the time of death flexible. If a specific, unchangeable time for our death were already set, the word *sterizo* ("fixed") or a similar word would have been used in Hebrews 9:27.

Considering the exception of the Rapture, of which Enoch is a type, death is approaching for each one of us.

We Do Not Have To Fear Death

A good friend of mine became so consumed with the fear of dying that he entered the medical field in an effort to avoid death's eventual grip. Death was a very fearful thing to him. Death is "the boogeyman" to many; they see it as a terrible, mysterious monster that is ready to gobble us up at any moment. Others try to befriend death through participation in various cults and cultic rituals — only to be duped by its grip. In most cases, involvement in such activities is nothing more than an expression of the fear of death.

But there is good news: We don't have to fear death! We are not left without answers, nor are we left without the opportunity to have confidence when death comes. The Apostle Paul wrote, "Behold, I shew you a mystery" (I Cor. 15:51), and "I would not have you to be ignorant" (I Thess. 4:13). In these instances, Paul was referring to death. The key phrases here are "shew you" and "do not be ignorant," which reveal that death is not a mystery; it is a ready revelation for all who will sincerely inquire.

According to Scripture, it was God's righteousness that demanded the severe penalty of death as a result of sin. Then it must be God who issues the remedy and healing for the fear and plight of death.

Watered-Down Ideas?

Someone who truly cares about your well-being will lovingly tell you the truth. Therefore, God, who loves the world (Jn. 3:16), does not provide sugar-coated or watered-down ideas. In His infinite love, He tells the truth. God is the very embodiment of truth (Titus 1:2). He lets us know that death will indeed bring glorious rewards to those who are prepared for it, but He also reveals that death will yield horrendous consequences for those who are not prepared. The outcome depends upon whether we have trusted God's plan concerning our lives and our futures.

Moreover, God's Word, the Bible, revolves around a Man who died, was buried, and resurrected three days later. His name is Jesus. All Old Testament writings point to Christ Jesus. An old adage concerning the Old and New Testaments goes something like this: "The New is in the Old contained and the Old is in the New explained." The New Testament brings the Old Testament to light in that the expected Messiah was fulfilled in Christ Jesus, the only begotten of God. It was Jesus who actually experienced death and arose from the dead three days later. It's this very same Jesus who ascended into heaven and has promised to return.

It must be noted that the death Jesus experienced was more than a near-death or an out-of-body phenomenon. His was a complete physical death, yet He arose. This would seem absurd to the natural man. How can someone be dead for three days and then arise to life? This is impossible, isn't it? It would be impossible if it were not for Jesus' amazing identity.

21

He is far more than a teacher, a philosopher or a redeemer, as many religions teach. Jesus is God who became flesh (Jn. 1:1–14) and who arose by His own power (Jn. 2:19–21). He is the Creator of all things (Col. 1:12–17).

Jesus' death was witnessed by multitudes. But the witness didn't stop there. He resurrected from the dead and revealed Himself to many. Jesus spent 40 days on the Earth during the time between His resurrection and His ascension into heaven (Acts 1:9–11). During this time, Jesus was seen by Mary Magdalene (Jn. 20:11–18); by other women (Matt. 28:9–10); by Cleophas and an unnamed disciple on the road to Emmaus, and again with the disciples (Lk. 24:13–35); by ten of the disciples — without Thomas (Jn. 20:19–25); and by the disciples with Thomas (Jn. 20:26–29). He was also seen again by Peter (Jn. 21:1–25). The resurrected Jesus breathed, walked, talked, ate, and was touched by human hands. He was also physically present at the Great Commission (Matt. 28:16–20); He was seen by 500 at one time (I Cor. 15:3–6) and He was seen ascending into heaven (Acts 1:4–11).

After the ascension, Jesus revealed himself to Paul, then called Saul, on the road to Damascus (Acts 9:3–6), and He later revealed Himself to John on the Isle of Patmos (Rev. 1:10–18).

We can trust Jesus through life, through death, and

through the events that follow. He has crossed the river of death and returned. He alone holds the keys of death (Rev. 1:18). This same Jesus became sin for us (II Cor. 5:21) and removed the sting from death on our behalf (I Cor. 15:55–56).

Death: A Result of Sin

Scripture reveals that death is a result of sin. God warned Adam to not eat of the forbidden fruit, stating that if he did he would die. "In the day thou eatest thereof thou shalt surely die" (Gen. 2:17). Adam *did* eat and was cursed with death (Rom. 6:23). The first aspect of human death was spiritual: separation from God. This separation, as well as physical death, was passed on to every individual from every generation (I Cor. 15:22). Thanks be to God that a way of escape has been made from the curse of sin and death.

Preparation for Death is a Must

We will see in later chapters that death should be greatly feared by those who aren't prepared. It is more than a mere passing of life; it is the doorway from the temporary to the eternal. This makes death very serious business. Preparation must be taken seriously and acted upon quickly.

"Turn to the Lord one day before you die," was the advice given by a sage to his followers. "And who can know the day of his death, Master?" asked one who heard his counsel. "True," said the sage, "and for that reason, you should turn to the Lord today, for you may die tomorrow" (see Proverbs 27:1).

23

Each of the following chapters is a piece of the puzzle that will enhance the overall understanding of what occurs when death comes. May God richly bless you as you study His Word. Ω

CHAPTER
2

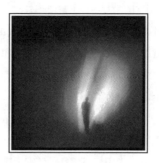

WE ARE
WONDERFULLY
MADE

Most of us have knowledge about everything
except the things that matter most.

In general, people are well aware of their family descent or personal goals. But most have no clue as to who they are, why they exist, or where they fit into the scheme of things. Knowing who we are and what makes us tick plays a very important role in our understanding of death and the afterlife.

Multitudes today are turning to various mediums in an attempt to understand self: psychology, self-help therapy, the internet, physical or emotional discipline, and so on. Some try to find inner peace through New Age practices such as astrology, the use of psychics, participation in witchcraft, or the following of priests or gurus. For the Christian, traveling down these avenues would be like going to an auto mechanic for heart surgery.

If we are honestly seeking self, then our search will eventually lead us to a great and awesome decision: accepting or rejecting the truth. We will find, or at least stumble across, the source, force and course for our lives: Creator God. It is then that we must decide to believe or not. That decision will affect us forever. Eternity is set before us at the point of our decision. At this fork in the road we must be very cautious. We were created with eternal properties. This means that our lives reach far beyond the realm of mere physical existence.

We Are Wonderfully Made
We are creatures who have properties that extend

far beyond the existence of flesh and blood. We are spirit beings as well as physical beings. The Apostle Paul revealed that humans are three-fold in nature; we consist of body, soul, and spirit (I Thess. 5:23). It is obvious then, that death affects more than mere physical existence.

Psalm 139:14 says that we are wonderfully made. The word "wonderfully" is *palah*, which means "to distinguish or set apart." This is only one of the many biblical examples that reveals that humans are set apart and different from all other creatures.

The first chapter of the Bible explains that God created us in His image and likeness (Gen. 1:26). Although plants, animals, and indeed all things are God's creation, no creatures besides humans carry the distinction of being created in God's image and likeness.

The word "image" in Genesis 1:26 is *tselem,* meaning "to shade; a phantom, a resemblance." The word "likeness" is *demuwth,* meaning "fashion; likeness; manner; similitude." These words relate that we are specially made for a specific reason. We have a unique existence. Humans are not exact copies of God, making us little gods, but we are similar to and patterned after the original. That's incredible!

It's obvious that "God's image and likeness" refers to more than outward, physical appearances. All we have to do is look around and see the various races, colors, sizes, shapes, and other aspects of human differences. God is no respecter of persons; therefore, we find that His image and likeness is not found in one particular race, nationality, size or shape. How then are we made in His image and likeness? The whole being of each individual is fashioned after God. Let's now consider God's wonderful and marvelous three-fold nature and being.

God's Three-fold Being

God is the one and only God (Eph. 4:4–6). However, Scripture reveals that He is three-fold in being. We find the first among many references for this principle in Genesis 1:1–3:

1. "In the beginning God" (Gen. 1:1). This reflects the Supreme being of Father God, who is above all things. The Hebrew word for God here is *'elohiym*. This word is in plural form and expresses that His being surpasses singularity. Note: This in no way suggests the idea of multiple gods, but that the being and existence of the One True God is plural.

2. "And the Spirit of God moved upon the face of the waters" (Gen. 1:2). This reveals that God is also Spirit (Gen. 1:2; Jn. 4:24).

3. In Genesis 1:3, God spoke, or, God "said." This verbalization is the "Word," or the "divine expression" of God (Gen. 1:3). This is the aspect of God's being that would later become flesh (Jn. 1:1–14). This flesh existence refers to none other than Jesus

28

Christ, the divine expression of God in human form, indeed, God in the flesh. This aspect of the Godhead excludes any other so-called redeemer or savior, for there is one "only begotten" of the Father (Jn. 1:14; 3:16). We must guard against imitations.

"Beware lest any man spoil you through philosophy and vain deceit, after the tradition of men, after the rudiments of the world, and not after Christ. For in him dwelleth all the fullness of the Godhead bodily" (Colossians 2:8–9).

The word "Godhead" is found only three times in Scripture (Acts 17:29; Rom. 1:20; Col. 2:9). Here, the Greek word used is *theotes*, which means "divinity." Thus, the fullness of the Godhead or the divinity of God dwells in Jesus. This reflects more than just having divine qualities. Jesus is God in the flesh (Jn. 1:14).

A familiar New Testament reference to God's three-fold being is found in Matthew 3:16–17 where we read about Jesus' baptism:

1. The Holy Spirit is seen descending from heaven;

2. The Father is heard speaking from heaven; and

3. Jesus is seen standing in the water with John (called the baptist). The Apostle John also records a wonderful witness to God's three-fold nature and oneness:

"For there are three that bear record in heaven, the **Father,** the **Word,** and the **Holy Ghost:** and these three are one" (I John 5:7).

Therefore, it is quite apparent that the one and only God is three-fold in being represented as the Supreme Father, the Word (Jesus), and the Holy Ghost (Spirit). That excludes Buddha, Mohammed, and Allah, as well as any other so-called avenue or appellation to and of God.

Our Image and Likeness

As seen earlier, human beings were created in the image and likeness of God. As God is three-fold in being, we too are three-fold in being. The Apostle Paul revealed this aspect in I Thessalonians 5:23:

> "And the very God of peace sanctify you **wholly**; and I pray God your whole **spirit** and **soul** and **body** be preserved blameless unto the coming of our Lord Jesus Christ" (I Thessalonians 5:23).

Again, we see that we are more than mere physical beings. We are also spirit and soul (Gen. 6:3).

It's important to note that the embodiment of God has been revealed in Scripture as three-fold in order that we may have knowledge of His nature, knowledge of His correspondence and likeness to mankind, and ultimately for an understanding of the fulfillment of His plan. The terms "Father," "Son," and "Holy Ghost" are also given for this purpose. In this light we may also relate to Him as a loving and compassionate Father. Note also that God will be "all in all" at the appointed time with the glory that existed long before the world (I Cor. 15:28; Jn. 17:5).

Note on Baptism: Understanding the three-in-one principle eliminates much confusion regarding the baptism of new converts. Some baptize in Jesus' name only, while others baptize in the name of the Father, Son, and the Holy Ghost. Either method is acceptable when applying proper knowledge of the Godhead (Col. 2:8–9). There are no contradictions in Scripture, as all Scripture is inspired by God (II Tim. 3:16). God is truth (Jn. 3:33), therefore He cannot lie (Titus 1:2; Heb. 6:18). Doing anything in the name of Jesus Christ is a virtual recognition of the Godhead. Jesus is the only begotten of the Father and the sender of the "other Comforter," which is the Holy Spirit (Col. 3:17).

Man's Eternal Soul

Although the word "soul" is used many times in the Old Testament to refer to physical life, it also refers to the inner life of man, the seat of his emotions, and the center of human personality. The first biblical mention of the soul expresses this meaning:

> "And the Lord God formed man of the dust of the ground, and breathed into his nostrils the breath of life; and man became a living soul" (Genesis 2:7).

Breathing life into man's nostrils reveals something far beyond the creation of mere physical existence. The life breathed into man induced the soul (man "became" a living soul). That is, God created man, then He breathed life into him. At that moment, man consisted of an inner man as well as an outer man and acquired the ability to think, feel and experience emotions.

Moreover, it was the soul, imparted from the eternal God, that caused man (Adam and his descendants) to exist as eternal creatures. This eternal aspect made man (after the fall) susceptible to one of two fates: eternal life or eternal death. Alongside the God-given ability to think and reason came the ability of personal choice.

Adam: Aware of Death

Adam was acutely aware of death because God had warned him not to eat of the forbidden fruit or else he would die:

"But of the tree of the knowledge of good and evil, thou shalt not eat of it: for in the day that thou eatest thereof thou shalt surely die" (Genesis 2:17).

Adam was not a humped-over, gorilla-like anthropoid without understanding. He had super intelligence. God had given him a mind that had the ability to name every creature (Gen. 2:19) and recall the names of each one. Such intelligence demands reason, subjection and an astute awareness of warnings and retribution. We, too, should cherish this God-given ability. Naturally, alongside our ability to reason comes the ability to choose — at the risk of choosing poorly. Care must accompany the choices we make, for what we think we know in our hearts may not always be correct.

The Heart of Man

It's easy to rely on feelings or emotions to express deep sentiment or spirituality. It's called "I-know-it-in-my-heart" idealism. However, many Scriptures warn us to "be not deceived." The sad truth is our hearts *can* deceive us and lead us astray.

The word "heart" appears in the New Testament approximately 105 times, while its plural form appears 61 times. Thus, there are 166 direct references to the heart in the New Testament alone. Only seven vary in some form from the word *kardia*, from where we get our English word "cardiac."

Although *kardia* may appear only to reflect the organ inside of our chests, it is most often used in Scripture to refer to man's entire being of body, soul and spirit. Therefore, the heart is the complete and intertwined three-fold being of man with all of its physical, spiritual and mental attributes and abilities.

Scripture relates that the heart may also refer to the middle or center of something, such as "the heart of the earth" (Matt. 12:40). It may also refer to "broken-heartedness" (Jn. 14:1;16:6); "hardness of the heart" (Matt. 19:8; Mrk. 10:5; 16:14); "hearts failing" (Lk. 21:26); and "knowest the heart" (Lk. 1:24; 15:8). Paul used the word *psuche* in Ephesians 6:6, which refers to the very breath and life-force within us.

Jesus gave a commandment concerning the heart of man and further breaks down the aspects of body, soul and spirit:

> "Jesus said unto him, Thou shalt love the Lord thy God with all thy heart, and with all thy soul, and with all thy mind. This is the first and great commandment" (Matthew 22:37–38).

We are to love the Lord with all of our hearts. The word for heart here is *kardia*, which, as seen above, refers to our entire three-fold being of body, soul and spirit. In addition, the Lord mentioned that we are to love Him with all of our souls, or *psuche*. Here *psuche* consists of the breath and sentiment of body and soul. We are also to love the Lord with all of our minds. The word for "mind" here is *dianoia*, which denotes the exercise of the mind, such as the thoughts and imagination. These aspects will be discussed in the following chapter.

Luke adds that we are to love the Lord with all of our strength, or *ischus* (Lk. 10:27). This consists of our physical and mental abilities, our might and power. Again, the heart of man is the complete, intertwined, three-fold being of man with all of the physical, spiritual and mental attributes and abilities. If we think we "know it in our hearts," then we must first "study to show [ourselves] approved" (II Tim. 2:15).

The Ability to Reason

The ability to reason necessitates correspondence

between the outer and inner man. This correspondence is orchestrated via doorways that connect the outer and inner aspects of our three-fold being. Understanding how this works helps eliminate confusion about life and death.

We have seen in this chapter that we are wonderfully made in the image and likeness of Almighty God. In the following chapter we will see how our outer and inner man work in concert to make us who and what we are. Ω

God Is Three-fold

In Being:

Father

Son (Jesus)

Holy Ghost (Spirit)

We Are Three-fold

In Being:

Body

Soul

Spirit

CHAPTER
3

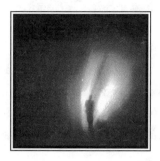

THE INNER
AND OUTER MAN

God gave us five senses: sight, hearing, taste,
touch, smell. Moreover, we have a sixth:
common sense.

This chapter is devoted to knowing ourselves. This encompasses more than being aware of our likes and dislikes, our strengths and weaknesses, or our limitations. It's more than knowing the human body and how it functions. It's understanding how our inner and outer man work in concert to constitute our entire being. Understanding self in this manner will greatly enhance our understanding of life, death, and the afterlife.

We must realize that death is not a portal to oblivion, for oblivion doesn't fit into the picture at all. Death is a doorway. There are also doorways between the inner and outer man: the five senses of the body.

Our Correspondence

Our five senses are the means by which we relate to the world around us. The senses of the body are: sight, hearing, taste, touch, and smell. These senses act as doorways by which the outer man (the body) corresponds with the inner man (spirit and soul).

The soul also has five senses: imagination, memory, reason, affection and consciousness. Correspondence from the outer man is received and computed through these senses. The senses of the soul work in harmony with the senses of the body as follows:

Body	Soul
sight	imagination
hearing	memory
taste	reason
touch	affection
smell	consciousness

38

Note: The following analogies are respectfully given under what is considered "normal" circumstances through which the senses of the body operate. God has provided amazing avenues and inventive techniques that allow for those who are physically impaired.

Sight – Imagination

The sense of sight corresponds with the inner sense of imagination. The things that we see cause us to think, dream, plan, and eventually work toward a goal. Even those who are physically blind can dream, imagine, and set goals of achievement. This is accomplished through imagination, the mind's eye.

Hearing – Memory

The sense of hearing corresponds with memory. The things we hear permeate our thoughts and remain there for recall and reference. How many times have we heard positive or negative things that remain with us throughout our lives? In this manner, hearing corresponds with memory.

Taste – Reason

The outer man tastes food and determines whether to swallow or spit it out. This computation of thought is the ability to reason, that is, to think and make judgments based upon experiences. In this manner, the doorway of taste works in concert with reason.

Smell – Consciousness

Many times one may find himself deep in thought, asleep or preoccupied in some fashion. Suddenly something happens and we are made aware of our surroundings. I am reminded of the time when I was driving along a country road, enjoying the sweet aroma of the honey-suckle blossom. This pleasantry ended abruptly when I saw and smelled a skunk that was nearby. I was very quickly made aware of my surroundings. Odors cause one to examine cause and effect and determine a situation. Such action is turned over to the response of reason. In this fashion, the sense of smell of the outer man corresponds to the inner sense of consciousness.

Looking at the World from the Outside In

More often than not, we allow the outer man to rule the inner man due to the things we take in through the senses of our bodies. This action is often explained in Scripture as walking or conducting oneself according to the flesh. It is very difficult for the inner man to bring the outer man into subjection because of the human spirit within. It is a natural spirit. This is where one must be born again (Jn. 3:7). That is, we must obtain a new life-changing spirit. This involves more than a change of attitude or a change of circumstance, as we will see shortly. When we allow our outer physical man to guide our actions, we become driven by the lust of the flesh; therefore, we are ruled from the outside inward. We have more trouble with this than anything else.

You Must Be Born Again

The term "born again" comes from the Greek term, *gennao anothen,* meaning to be "born from above." It is a spiritual rebirth. The wonder of true, spiritual rebirth can only be obtained through the avenue provided by the Creator.

Many false ideas have arisen about how one is to be "born again." Religion (different from Christianity) stresses that salvation and spiritual rebirth occur through one's good works. Such thoughts stem from the natural spirit within, the source from which all heresy arises. The natural spirit within is what makes us a "natural" man. When thinking upon spiritual things, the natural man is at a great loss. Consider what the Apostle Paul wrote:

> "But the natural man receiveth not the things of the Spirit of God: for they are foolishness unto him: neither can he know them, because they are spiritually discerned" (I Corinthians 2:14).

The Natural Spirit Within

Nicodemus, a ruler of Israel and devout religious man, came to Jesus with concerns about salvation (Jn. 3). Jesus told Nicodemus that a man cannot see or enter the kingdom of God without becoming born again. The puzzled Nicodemus responded through his

41

natural human spirit:

> Nicodemus saith unto him, **How can a man be born when he is old? can he enter the second time into his mother's womb, and be born?** Jesus answered, Verily, verily, I say unto thee, Except a man be born of water and of the Spirit, he cannot enter into the kingdom of God. That which is born of the flesh is flesh; and that which is born of the Spirit is spirit (John 3:4–6).

Jesus considered the existence of angels and other created things when He affirmed that one must first be born naturally (physical birth — born of water). That is to say, it is absolutely necessary that we are born into the physical realm before we can be born of the Spirit (born "again"). This is one reason that angels desire to understand salvation (I Peter 1:9–12). Angels cannot experience salvation because they have never been born into the physical realm. (For more on the natural birth of angelic creatures, see the author's book, *The Unveiling,* pgs. 182–184,198, under the subheadings "Bottomless Pit" and "Demons," respectively).

Again, the natural man is born with a natural human spirit. That's what makes him a natural man. Therefore, it is a must that the natural man be born again of the Holy Spirit.

In the passages above, we see that spiritual rebirth does not come by water baptism, as many conclude. The reference to being born of water is clearly connected to the natural birthing process. This is realized by the question Nicodemus asked and was affirmed by Jesus' reply in verse 6: "That which is born of the flesh is flesh; and that which is born of the Spirit is spirit." We must not make more of what is written than what is obviously intended.

When man is born into this world, he arrives equipped with a natural human spirit, a life-force. The infantile physical body feeds this natural spirit according to genealogical and environmental conditions. The natural spirit within grows into the part of man that orchestrates correspondence between body and soul. Thus, the soul computes the conditions of life by way of the natural spirit. This is what makes man a natural man. In one form or another, this is evidenced by the deeds of the body. Therefore, it is absolutely necessary that a person become "born again" of the Holy Spirit of God. Again, the natural man cannot know the things of the Spirit of God (I Cor. 2:14; Jn. 6:44).

Understanding from the Inside Out

The spiritual rebirth is known as *salvation*, one of the aspects of becoming born again. When a person is born again, his soul is saved from the curse of sin brought upon man by Adam (Rom. 5:12). Salvation is brought about first by the soul's reasoning ability to rightly apply his God-given faith in Jesus Christ as Lord and Savior (Jn. 6:44).

After a person is "born again," the soul is no longer governed by the deeds of a body driven by a natural spirit. The soul is now driven by a new spirit within, the Holy Spirit. Thus, the soul is no longer governed from the outside in, but from the inside out. That is, a person no longer looks at the world through his natural eye (looking from the outside in), but through his spiritual eye (looking from the inside out). This is why the world appears brand new after we become born again.

Scripture explains that we must be born again. If the new birth does not occur, man will remain under the curse of sin. This curse brings physical, spiritual, and eternal death. Many men have confused the issues of Christianity by interpreting Scripture without ever coming to Christ for salvation. A person is prone to interpret life's complexities by using many ideas that are totally against God's plan and design when he remains a natural man. This is evidenced in such ideas and practices as evolution, homosexuality, abortion, and near-death phenomena (non-biblical).

Self-Salvation

Changing our attitude, performing good deeds, or trying to use any avenue other than the one God has provided will never produce a biblical and spiritual rebirth.

> "Not by works of righteousness which we have done, but according to his mercy he saved us, by the washing of regeneration, and renewing of the Holy Ghost; Which he shed on us abundantly through Jesus Christ our Saviour; That being

justified by his grace, we should be made heirs according to the hope of eternal life" (Titus 3:5–7).

In order to receive salvation and enter the kingdom of God, we must have the spiritual rebirth as designed by Creator God through Jesus Christ. Contentment and true happiness will only flow through life when we are fed from something other than our natural spirit. Let's face it, we cannot save ourselves! Jesus revealed the good news about salvation to Nicodemus:

> "That whosoever believeth in him (Jesus) should not perish, but have eternal life. For God so loved the world, that he gave his only begotten Son, that whosoever believeth in him should not perish, but have everlasting life. For God sent not his Son into the world to condemn the world; but that the world through him might be saved" (John 3:15–17).

The Apostle Paul also revealed the road to receiving the new God-given, life-changing Spirit. We must understand the following realities: no one is righteous (Rom. 3:10); all are sinners (Rom. 3:23); all are sinners because of Adam's transgression (Rom. 5:12); there is a terrible result for sin (Rom. 6:23); God has great concern for sinners (Rom. 5:8); God's way of salvation is made plain (Rom. 10: 9–10); and whosoever call's upon the name of the Lord has the assurance of salvation (Rom. 10:13). True commitment will then be followed by outward evidences beginning with water baptism and fellowship with other believers. Water baptism is the outer sign of an inner occurrence (Matt.

28:19; I Peter 3:21). Fellowship with other believers is a requirement for spiritual growth (Heb. 10:25–26).

Soul salvation will generate new revelations about life and will produce lasting peace and satisfaction. Everything will become new (II Cor. 5:17). Death will also take on new meaning (Psa. 116:15; Phil. 1:21).

Evidences of the New Spirit Within

The person who becomes born again of the Spirit becomes a new creature. The actions of the body take on new life and new direction due to the new Spirit who resides within the believer. We must keep in mind that the new Spirit within is a supernatural Spirit living in a natural body. Therefore, we cannot expect to immediately become perfect in every deed or action. Nor can we expect the actions of other Christians to be perfect (Gal. 5:16–18; 6:1–2). However, we are to grow spiritually and mature in Christ (II Peter 3:17–18). This requires a daily walk with Christ through a study of biblical principles. By abiding in God's Word we allow the Holy Spirit to guide us, remembering that we are apt to stumble (I Jn. 1:8–2:6) when we are tempted by the natural spirit (James 1:14–15). Christian maturity is evidenced by character and action.

Looking from the Inside Out

The reason one becomes a new creature is that the spirit within stems from a totally different source: the

Holy Spirit of God. Therefore, instead of looking at the world through our physical senses — from the outside in — the new Spirit takes over and the world is viewed from the inside out.

The Five Senses of the New Spirit

The senses of the old human spirit will naturally plunge one into a jumbled mess of ideas and actions apart from the will of God. It is a natural, physically driven spirit. However, the person who has experienced spiritual rebirth through the Holy Spirit will take on a new nature due to the Spirit's indwelling. The five senses of the human spirit are thus brought into perspective and align themselves with the senses of the soul and body to make a person whole. The five senses of the new human spirit are: hope, faith, love, prayer, and worship. They work in conjunction with the body and soul as follows:

body	soul	spirit
sight	imagination	hope
hearing	memory	faith
taste	reason	love
touch	affection	prayer
smell	consciousness	worship

Sight – Imagination and Hope

"For we are saved by hope: but hope that is seen is not hope: for what a man seeth, why doth he yet hope for? But if we hope for that we see not, then do we with patience wait for it" (Romans 8:24–25).

47

The natural man looks at the world from the out-side in and cannot know the things of God (I Cor. 2:14). However, the new man looks at the world from the inside out. Therefore, the spiritual sense of hope looks through the mind's eye and visualizes things that one day will be experienced physically as well as spir-itually. This is called hope. In this way, hope aligns with the sense of imagination, and when brought into perspective, aligns with the sense of sight (that is, look-ing from the inside out).

"(For we walk by faith, not by [physical] sight:)" (II Corinthians 5:7).

Hearing – Memory and Faith

Christ dwells in the heart of the Christian by faith and is strengthened by the Spirit of God (Eph. 3:16–17). In addition, we know that faith comes by hearing and hearing by the Word of God (Rom. 10:17). The Apostle Paul wrote that "though our outward man perish, the inward man is renewed day by day" (II Cor. 4:16). This involves the renewing of the mind (Eph. 4:23–24). In this fashion, faith, memory and hearing are interconnected and brought into perspective:

"Jesus said unto him, Thou shalt love the Lord thy God with all thy heart, and with all thy soul, and with **all thy mind**" (Matthew 22:37).

Taste – Reason and Love

We saw earlier that taste is connected with reason.

We have also seen that a person can think and make judgments based upon things that have been experienced. In like manner, love is not an overwhelming dragon that forces us to have affection toward something or someone. Love is a blossoming choice based upon the yearnings of the inner man. We must allow godly love to rule us.

"Let all your things be done with charity (*agape* – love)" (I Corinthians 16:14) (emphasis from the Greek).

Love is a judgment whose reigns we are privileged to loosen that it may overwhelm us, but only in the Lord. There are ten Greek words translated as "love" in the New Testament. They are:

1. *Agapao:* to love in a social or moral sense.
2. *Agape:* an affectionate love-feast; dearly, charitably.
3. *Thelo:* to determine as an act, option; impulse, to wish, be inclined to.
4. *Phileo:* to be a friend; have affection for (denoting personal attachment as a matter of sentiment or feeling).
5. *Philadelphia:* fraternal affection; brotherly love.
6. *Philarguria:* avarice; love of money.
7. *Philandros:* fond of man; affectionate as a wife.
8. *Philoteknos:* fond of one's children; maternal.
9. *Philanthropia:* fondness or kindness toward man.
10. *Philadelphos:* fond of brethren; fraternal.

The born-again person has the ability to reason what is good, bad, right or wrong. The Holy Spirit within guides the love and affection of the born-again person; he will grow in grace and knowledge (I Peter 2:2–3). Therefore, those who are born again will love God affectionately, dearly and charitably.

"Love (*agapao*) not the world, neither the things that are in the world. If any man love (*agapao*) the world, the love (*agape*) of the Father is not in him" (I John 2:15) (emphasis from Greek).

Touch – Affection and Prayer

"If ye then be risen with Christ, seek those things which are above, where Christ sitteth on the right hand of God. Set your affection on things above, not on things on the earth" (Colossians 3:1–2).

Reaching (touching) heaven through prayer is a wonderful privilege. In turn, heaven touches us. This comes only by setting our affections upon the things above through prayer.

"Praying always with all prayer and supplication in the Spirit, and watching thereunto with all perseverance and supplication for all saints" (Ephesians 6:18).

Smell – Consciousness and Worship

A sacrifice is seen as a sweet-smelling savor (*reyach* – scent, smell) to the Lord in the Old Testament (Gen. 8:21). This is pleasant for God. In the New Testament, we read that Christians are to be pleasant to God as a sweet-smelling savor.

> "For we are unto God a sweet savour (*euodia*: good fragrance) of Christ, in them that are saved" (II Corinthians 2:15).

A blood sacrifice was necessary to cover sin under Old Testament Law. This was to be done until the time of Christ's ultimate sacrifice. Sacrifices were a great part of worshiping God in that they pointed to Christ's death on the cross. Offering the blood of bulls and goats has been unnecessary and ineffective since Jesus' sacrifice for sin. There is, however, a request for sacrifice — we are to be "living sacrifices" for God through Christ.

> "I beseech you therefore, brethren, by the mercies of God, that ye present your bodies **a living sacrifice,** holy, acceptable unto God, which is your reasonable service" (Romans 12:1).

Offering our lives for the cause of Christ necessitates true worship. Worship, in turn, demands a consciousness of whom or what is being worshiped. Therefore, as a sweet smelling savor (II Cor. 2:15) and a living sacrifice for Christ, we understand the connection between the sense of smell and its branches: consciousness and worship.

> "God is a Spirit: and they that worship him must worship him in spirit and in truth" (John 4:24).

Putting our three-fold nature into perspective plays an important role in developing an understanding of life, death, and what is termed as the "afterlife." In the following chapters, we will reveal how the body, soul, and spirit are separated at death. But before we venture into a discussion of this aspect of our being, it is necessary to put another piece of the life-and-death puzzle in its place. As each piece of the puzzle comes together, we begin to see more and more of the biblical picture of death unfold before us. Ω

Our Interconnected Three-fold Being

Body	Soul	Spirit
sight	imagination	hope
hearing	memory	faith
taste	reason	love
touch	affection	prayer
smell	consciousness	worship

CHAPTER 4

GOD'S
OVERALL PLAN

To undertake the subject of death and the
afterlife without including God's overall plan
would be like making a Hershey chocolate bar
and leaving out the chocolate.

This chapter deals with the chronology of dispensations beginning with Adam and ending with our eternal home: the new heaven and new Earth. Such a study may seem out of order and unnecessary for the subject at hand; however, the lack of such teaching has bred confusion, fantasy, and out-and-out heresy concerning death and the afterlife. Knowing God's overall plan is a must concerning any biblical study.

The following explanations are concise but necessary in order to solve the puzzle of death and the things that follow. One important truth is that those who died prior to the cross of Calvary (under Old Testament Law) were dealt with differently than those who have died after Calvary. This same principle applies to those who will die after the Rapture of the Church, during the Tribulation Period and so on. These differences must be reconciled; therefore, the need for this chapter will be made clear as our study continues.

Time of Innocence

Since Adam, God has dealt with mankind through the progression of history to bring all things to fulfillment according to His Word. God has always given man a choice to accept or reject His direction. This has been the case from the very onset of man's existence in the Garden of Eden. The Garden Period was a time of innocence supplied with choice.

The period of innocence lasted until Adam sinned against God and was removed from the Garden. Adam and Eve had enjoyed access to every tree except one; therefore, choice did exist. Through the devil's deception, Adam chose to disobey God and eat the fruit of the forbidden tree. Therefore, all have been born under the curse of sin since Adam. It was then that death became a sentence for man (Rom. 5:12–17). What began with spiritual death was followed by physical death (Rom. 6:23). Until that time, physical death was only a part of nature and was not imputed to man (Rom. 5:12–13). (Note: for more on the law of sin, see the author's book, *Jurassic Mark*.)

Age of Personal Responsibility

Adam and Eve's expulsion from the Garden brought an age of personal responsibility. The sentence would be immediately realized through labor: the sweat of the brow and pain in childbirth (Gen. 3:16,19). Not only was God's grace and mercy known because of the Garden experience, but also the plight of disobeying God was known due to Adam's sin. Man's conscience would be his guide during this time. Also during this age of responsibility, Adam's firstborn son, Cain, killed his brother, Abel.

Abel was the first human to die because of sin; however, God continued a godly lineage through another son of Adam and Eve: Seth. Through this lineage Christ later came to Earth.

As punishment for his sin, Cain was cast away from the family and left to become a fugitive and a vagabond (Gen. 4:12). God put a mark (*owth* [as in appearance], as that of a beacon) on Cain for recognition, for shunning, and for his protection (Gen. 4:15). Cain's expulsion and mark also stood as a reminder of God's punishment against sin. Thus, those attributes both pleasing and displeasing to God would be known during this age of responsibility.

Flood of Noah

Due to the flourishing population and the working of evil in the hearts of men, corruption and degradation abounded after Adam and Eve's expulsion from the Garden of Eden. Man's lack of self-discipline during the age of responsibility caused the searing of the conscience. Man became self-reliant. Disrespect for God's principles continued. Such sin brought the necessary cleansing of the Earth, which came by flood. Noah, a descendant of Adam through his son Seth, found grace in the eyes of the Lord and was spared this terrible judgment.

The Bible clearly reveals that only eight individuals survived the flood of Noah's time (I Peter 3:20). This deluge covered the entire Earth and wiped out all forms of life (Gen. 6:17) except Noah, his family, the chosen animals in the ark, and the sea creatures. God made a covenant with Noah that the Earth would never again be flooded by water (Gen. 9:9). God gave a rainbow as a sign of that covenant (Gen. 9:13).

The Age of Man's Covenant

A great rebellion against the God of Noah was headed by Nimrod, a descendant of Noah through his son Ham. This was the time of the infamous Tower of Babel and the confusion of languages. However, a godly lineage continued through Noah's son, Shem.

Through Shem's lineage came a man called Abram ("high father"), whose name God later changed to Abraham ("father of a multitude" — Gen. 17:5). The age of God's covenant with mankind for eternal purposes began with Abram (Gen. 15:18; 17:4,7; Gal. 3:7). He became a great man of faith. His father, Terah, was an idolater (Josh. 24:2), yet Abram purposed to follow the one and only God (Gen. 12:1–3).

Abram later came to be recognized as the father of nations (people of God), thus the name Abraham. It was his faith that was recognized by the people of God throughout history. After his death, Old Testament saints called the destination of the faithful dead "Abraham's bosom" (Lk. 16:22). This was a tender expression of laying one's head on the bosom of a caring and loving father. The children of Israel came through Abraham's grandson, Jacob and his sons.

The Age of the Law

Abraham's descendants fell under Egyptian bondage due to the process of sin. During this time

Moses was born. He later led the Hebrew children (called Hebrews as the descendants of Eber through Abraham) from this bondage. After the escape from bondage came the necessity for the Law. This Law was given to direct the people and was necessary because of sin (Gal. 3:19). *Nelson's Bible Dictionary* defines the Law as:

> An orderly system of rules and regulations by which a society is governed. In the Bible, particularly the Old Testament, a unique law code was established by direct revelation from God to direct His people in their worship, in their relationship to Him, and in their social relationships with one another.

The Age of Ultimate Responsibility

> "And the times of this ignorance God winked at; **but now commandeth all men every where to repent:** Because he hath appointed a day, in the which he will judge the world in righteousness by that man whom he hath ordained; whereof he hath given assurance unto all men, in that he hath raised him from the dead" (Acts 17:30–31).

The age of ultimate responsibility refers to the time extending from the Day of Pentecost until the "catching away" of the Church (called the Rapture). This period of time is also known as the Church Age. (However, an apostate church will continue after the Rapture of the true Church.)

The Law ended in Christ Jesus. He came not to destroy (demolish) the Law, but to fulfill it (Matt. 5:17). The Law is now our schoolmaster that brings the people of God to Christ Jesus (Gal. 3:24–25). Christ came to Earth to be the ultimate sacrifice for man, the only way by which he could be freed from the curse of sin and death (I Cor. 15:21–22). Salvation was offered because of grace.

Nelson's Bible Dictionary defines grace as:

Favor or kindness shown without regard to the worth or merit of the one who receives it and in spite of what that same person deserves. Grace is one of the key attributes of God. The Lord God is "merciful and gracious, long-suffering, and abounding in goodness and truth" (Ex. 34:6). Therefore, grace is almost always associated with mercy, love, compassion, and patience as the source of help and with deliverance from distress.

This day of grace, the Church Age, is also an age of ultimate responsibility. The responsibility lies in accepting Jesus Christ as Lord and Savior and living a life exemplary of that profession. We become responsible for our own fate if we do not accept God's plan through Jesus. The only exclusion is that of infants and those who are incapable of making that choice (discussed later). If one is not with Christ, he is against Christ (Matt. 12:30; Lk. 11:23). To steadfastly refuse

Him is the unpardonable sin (Matt. 12:31). We must not ignore the Spirit's urging. Jesus said:

> "He that is not with me is against me; and he that gathereth not with me scattereth abroad. Wherefore I say unto you, All manner of sin and blasphemy shall be forgiven unto men: but the blasphemy against the Holy Ghost shall not be forgiven unto men" (Matthew 12:30–31).

Christ's death, burial, resurrection and ascension have assured life for all those who call upon His name. The age of responsibility describes the time when "...whosoever shall call upon the name of the Lord [Jesus] shall be saved" (Rom. 3:10,13; 3:23; 5:12; 6:23; 5:8; 10:9,10,13). We are now living in this age of responsibility awaiting the return of our Lord. This necessitates a future plan. There are many viewpoints of God's chronology for future events; however, the most scholarly, most biblical, and most accepted order for these events are as follows:

The Rapture

The next major event for Christians will be the "catching away" commonly called the Rapture (I Thess. 4:17).

The Rapture will occur seven years prior to the Second Coming of Christ (Dan. 9:24–27; Rev. 19:11). The Bible gives us no signs preceeding the Rapture; however, many passages of Scripture indicate that it will happen at any moment (Matt. 24:36; Lk. 21:36; I Thess. 4:17; Rev. 3:10). All Christians who have died after the Day of Pentecost and before the Rapture will be included in this event (I Thess. 4:13–17); that is, the resurrection of the saints will occur at the Rapture.

Many try to dispel the reality of the Rapture by pointing out the absence of the word in the Bible. The word "rapture" comes from the Latin word *rapera,* which means to be "caught up." As seen above, this term is used in I Thessalonians 4:17: "Then we which are alive and remain shall be *caught up* together...." The Greek word is *harpazo.* The New Testament was originally written in Greek, however, very few people today can relate to being *harpazoed,* but most everyone can relate to being raptured in one form or another. Hence, the use of the term "rapture." Those who miss the Rapture, by reason of rejecting Christ as Lord, will be left behind to face seven years of the most terrible events in Earth's and mankind's history. This time is called the Tribulation Period (Matt. 24:21). Please prepare to miss this awful time (Lk. 21:36).

The Judgment Seat of Christ

This judgment will be for believers only and is not to be confused with the Great White Throne Judgment, which is reserved for unbelievers. The unbelievers' judgment will be after the Millennial Reign of Christ (discussed shortly).

The Judgment Seat of Christ immediately follows, or will occur in conjunction with the Rapture (I Cor.

3:11–17; I Cor. 15:52; II Cor. 5:10). (See author's
book, *The Unveiling*, for a full explanation of the
Judgment Seat of Christ as well as discussion of all
other prophetic aspects given in this book).

The Marriage Supper of the Lamb

This event will be for believers only and will occur
in heaven after the Rapture, after the Judgment Seat of
Christ, and before the Second Coming of Jesus Christ
to Earth (Rev. 19:7–9). This time frame is realized
because the Church ("caught out" believers) will
return to Earth with Christ (Zech. 14:5; Col. 3:4; I
Thess. 3:13; Jude 14; Rev. 19:7–9). Then the Bride of
Christ (II Cor. 11:2) will be represented by the term
"wife" (Rev. 19:7).

The Second Coming of Christ

This event is to be distinguished from the Rapture
of the Church. At the Rapture, born-again believers in
Jesus will be caught up to meet the Lord in the air. The
Second Coming of Christ is when Christ will split the
eastern sky and return to Earth to set up His kingdom.
It will be the most glorious event the world has ever
seen (Rev. 19:11). Christians will rule and reign with
Christ during the earthly kingdom (II Tim. 2:21; Rev.
20:6).

The Judgment of Nations

This event will take place after the Second Coming
of Christ to Earth. It will be for those left on Earth at

the Rapture. Those who are left behind after the Rapture will experience a seven-year period called the Tribulation, the most terrible time the world has ever known. The judgment of nations will occur after the Tribulation Period and after the Second Coming of Christ.

This judgment will be directed toward the nations of people on Earth who help or do not help the children of Israel during the Tribulation Period, also called the time of "Jacob's Trouble" (Jer. 30:7), because it is directed toward bringing the children of Israel to repentance. God has given His word that He will bring them back (Ezek. 16:8; 34:13–16). God always keeps His Word.

Those judged at this event either will be cast into Hades or allowed to enter into the Millennial Reign, depending upon their actions toward "my brethren" (Matt. 25: 31–46). Those who aid the children of Israel (Jews) are represented as sheep in Matthew's Gospel account and those who do not help the Jews are represented by goats. Again, this judgment will occur immediately after the Lord comes to the Earth to set up His earthly kingdom (Matt. 25:31; Lk. 1:32).

The Millennial Reign of Christ

This is the period when Christ Jesus will rule and reign upon the Earth from Jerusalem for 1,000 years (Lk. 1:32–33; Rev. 20:2–5). Present-day believers in Jesus Christ who are taken in the Rapture will rule and reign with Him (Rom. 8:17; II Tim. 2:12).

The term "millennium" has overshadowed the term "kingdom." This is due to the mention of only the length of this period in Scripture, that is, the "one thousand years" of Revelation 20:1–5. The term is also used to minimize confusion between the spiritual and literal kingdoms of Christ.

The Millennial Reign and the Kingdom have often been treated interchangeably. They are so called because Christ will set up a divine government on Earth over the nations of the world. It is the "thy kingdom come" of Matthew 6:10. This is in no way related to the kingdom portrayed by Jehovah's Witnesses (see the author's book, *The Unveiling*). This Earth will be set on fire after the Millennial Reign of Christ.

The Earth Will Be Cleansed by Fire

This will be the purification of the Earth for its eternal state (II Peter 3:10) after the Millennial Reign. After the Earth's cleansing by fire, the new city, New Jerusalem, will sit upon the newly cleansed Earth and will become our eternal home (Jn. 14:1–4). The Earth will be free from all sin (II Peter 3:10; Rev. 22:14–15). It is presently held in reserve for this day of cleansing (II Peter 3:7). Despite contrary belief, the Earth we now enjoy is established forever (Psa. 78:69; Eccl. 1:4). Therefore, it will not be annihilated, but will be changed from one condition to another. This is seen in the Greek word *parerchoma,* which is translated "passed away" in the King James Bible.

The New Heaven and the New Earth

The Earth, which will have been cleansed by fire, will be a purified place prepared for the New Jerusalem. It will once again flourish with vegetation and life. The heavens will also be purified and made new. The new heaven, new Earth and new city will be ours to enjoy for eternity (Rom. 8:31). It will be a wonderful place (Rev. 21–22).

It must be noted that those who have rejected God's plan will be excluded from the events mentioned beginning with the Rapture. They will be found in Hades awaiting their judgment at the Great White Throne. This is the judgment for unbelievers.

Perspective

The aspects discussed in this chapter have only covered the highlights of God's overall plan. We must know that we are not traveling through history in a helter-skelter fashion. God's Word reveals order and direction, which includes death and the afterlife. Not one person is excluded from God's order of things to come.

It becomes quite obvious that the different aspects of God's plan necessitate a coming together of the events of death for both Old and New Testament saints, that is, those who die before and after the cross of Christ. But what about those of the Church Age who die prior to the Rapture, those who are taken in the Rapture, and those who die after the Rapture? This we will learn in the next two chapters. We will also find out how we, as three-fold beings, become separated at death; what occurs between death and the resurrection; and where our residence will be immediately following death. Exploring these aspects of God's plan will drastically enhance our picture of death. Ω

CHAPTER
5

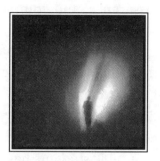

DESTINATIONS
PART 1: HEAVEN

Just about everybody believes in heaven. Some
live in denial by claiming to be atheists; however,
this does not change the facts, nor do I find that
God believes in atheists.

There are those who believe that heaven is a blissful place while others believe that heaven is here and now and nothing more. The Christian knows that God's Word holds the truth of the matter. If we are not afraid of the truth, it is ours for rest, peace, assurance, and complete freedom (Jn. 8:32).

The secular world has offered many ideas about heaven and hell through television, computer media and a myriad of other venues. Is it any wonder that we question, as did David of old, "Why do the heathen rage, and the people imagine a vain thing?" (Psa. 2:1) The lack of diligent Bible students has added greatly to this dilemma. Psalm 2:3 reveals the secularist goal:

"Let us break their bands asunder, and cast away their cords from us" (Psalm 2:3).

It would be easy to dismiss the literal existence of heaven or hell if you could totally dismiss the existence and validity of God's Word. Anyone who has a sincere desire for truth cannot do that. No written work has been as greatly substantiated, tested, and found to be inerrant as God's Word. God is so intent on telling us the truth that He had it written down for inspection and judgment. It's called the Bible.

It's easy to invest time in other interests and let God's Word gather dust. It's also easy to rely on others to rationalize what we want to hear and believe. The sad fact is, we have rested in hear-say for much too long. It's time to become personally involved and cast away the cords of the wicked for ourselves. We are to study God's Word for personal benefit and for truth (II Tim. 2:15).

The Destination of Heaven

If one believes in God, one must also believe in heaven, for that is where God dwells (Lk. 11:2). Angels dwell in heaven (Matt. 18:10). As he was being stoned, Stephen looked up into heaven and saw the glory of God (Acts 7:55). The Apostle John was caught up into heaven (Rev. 4:1).

The fact that the heaven where God dwells may be inter-dimensional and presently out of view does not dispel its existence. "Heaven is my throne, and Earth is my footstool: what house will ye build me? saith the Lord: or what is the place of my rest?" (Acts 7:49). It is in heaven that we are to lay up our treasures (Matt. 6:19–20).

The word "heaven" occurs approximately 143 times in the four Gospel accounts alone. The majority of these references came from Jesus' lips. To disbelieve in heaven is to call Jesus a liar (Rom. 3:4). If Jesus is true, and He is, then these utterances prove that heaven is an actual place: "Our Father which art in heaven" (Matt. 6:9,14); "things in heaven" (Jn. 3:12); "powers of heaven" (Mrk. 13:25); "angels of heaven" (Mrk. 13:32); "bread from heaven" (Jn. 6:31–32); "sinned against heaven" (Lk. 15:18). So heaven is

69

more than mere speculation and more than an ethereal fantasy-land. It's a real place with real characters.

God to Dwell with Man

The heaven where God currently dwells is "up" (Rev. 4:1). It is into this heaven that born-again believers will be "caught up" at the Rapture of the Church.

Many songs and messages from the pulpit express that we will live "up there forever." This may come as a surprise to many, but "up there somewhere" is not where our eternal home is located. Our eternal dwelling will be in the new city, New Jerusalem, which will be on the newly purified Earth (Rev. 21:3; II Peter 3:7).

The Church (born-again believers) will return to Earth with Christ approximately seven years after the Rapture (Zech. 14:5; Col. 3:4; I Thess. 3:13; Jude 14). There we will rule and reign with Him for 1,000 years, as seen in Chapter Four. It is the period called the "Millennial Reign" (I Cor. 15:25; II Tim. 2:12; Rev. 5:10; 20:16). The Earth will be purified by fire after the Millennial Reign (II Peter 3:10). God will dwell with man on the newly purified Earth in the New Jerusalem (Rev. 21:3), a literal city on a literal Earth, this Earth.

"And I heard a great voice out of heaven saying, Behold, **the tabernacle of God is with men,** and **he will dwell with them,** and they shall be his people, and God himself shall be with them, and be their God" (Revelation 21:3).

70

There is controversy today about whether heaven is a state of being or an actual place. It is both. It is a literal place and a blissful place. It is the "Father's house," a place with many mansions. It is the place that Jesus has gone away to prepare (Matt. 14:1–6). It is the new city, New Jerusalem. This place will be heavenly because God will be there. It will be physical and spiritual. Our existence, as well as our new home, will be much more than a mere ethereal existence.

Note: The Earth will not be annihilated by fire, as some believe. The Greek for "passed away" in II Peter 3:10,12, where this burning of the Earth by fire is found, is *parerchomai*. In short, this word means "to change from one condition to another." This change will occur when the Earth is burned and purified by fire (global warming?).

Three Heavens

When referring to heaven, Scripture relates that there are three: the atmospheric heaven surrounding the Earth, the heaven of the universe, and the third heaven, where God currently dwells. The third heaven, a paradise (II Cor. 12:4), is where Paul was caught up (II Cor. 12:2). John was also caught up into the third heaven (Rev. 4:1).

We have just seen that God will dwell with man in the heavenly place called New Jerusalem. It will exist on the Earth surrounded by the newly purified atmospheric heaven.

Where Do Christians Go Now When They Die?

The new city, New Jerusalem, will exist as the habitation of believers in Christ. This will be after the Second Coming, after the Millennial Reign and after the Earth is purified by fire. We know that these aspects of God's plan are yet future. The question is, "Where do Christians go now when they die?"

We read in Chapters Two and Three that each individual consists of a body, a soul, and a spirit. We have also seen that God is three-fold in being. Although crudely described herein, we have found that God divided Himself for the benefit of man's relationship to Him and for the fulfillment of His plan. He is revealed as Father, Son, and Holy Ghost. When Christians and non-Christians alike die, our bodies, souls, and spirits become divided or separated. This is a part of God's plan for man. Scripture relates that:

1. The body returns to the dust of the Earth (Gen. 3:19; Job 34:15; Psa. 104:29). The body ceases to function as a living, thinking being.

"His breath goeth forth, he returneth to his earth; in that very day his thoughts perish" (Psalm 146:4).

The word for "thoughts" here is *eshtonah* and means "thinking." The Greek word for "perish" is *abad*, which means "to wander away." This reveals that the thoughts leave the body when the spirit and soul leaves. It in no way suggests that the soul and spirit die.

2. The spirit or life-force of the body goes back to God who gave it (Eccl. 12:7). This spirit or life-force is temporary. Scripture bears witness to this (Gen. 6:3), as do cemeteries. The spirit here is the life-force of the body, the natural spirit, and separate from the Holy Spirit, which dwells in the heart of born-again individuals and is eternal.

3. The soul of the believer is redeemed by God (Psa. 49:15). The soul is taken to the place of perfect peace and rest to a sea of tranquility called the "Sea of Glass" (discussed later), a destination for the saved prior to the eternal and heavenly bliss of the New Jerusalem. This destination is the temporary dwelling place that exists for the saved between death and the resurrection. The soul, the seat of human emotion and thought, continues to exist in this state of bliss. Again, this is where the Christian soul goes at death prior to the Rapture of the Church. The soul will remain there until the resurrection (at the Rapture). The soul contains within its make-up all the feelings, thoughts, and presence of the body, but it is separated from the body at death. The only exception is the souls of those who are alive at the Rapture of the Church (I Cor.

73

15:51–52).

The Lost

Those who have not accepted God's plan for eternal life are referred to as "the lost." At death, their souls are delivered to Hades, a place of untold misery (Lk. 16:23). They are the "dead" of Revelation 20:13–14. These "dead" individuals include all those who have died and are now dying without having accepted God's plan of escape. The souls of the dead (of Hades) will be reunited with their bodies and judged at the Great White Throne Judgment (Rev. 20:11–15). Then the soul and body will be cast into *gehenna* hell (Matt. 10:28). This occurrence is the second death (Rev. 20:12–15) and will be dealt with more thoroughly in Chapter Six.

The Sea of Glass

To the Christian, death is referred to as "sleep" (I Cor. 11:30; 15:51; I Thess. 4:14; 5:10). This is not to be confused with the heresy known as "Soul Sleep" (discussed shortly).

The term "sleep" for the Christian is not only symbolic of death, but it also refers to a literal rest (Heb. 4:8–11). The Sea of Glass in Revelation 4:6 is the only place in Scripture that fits the biblical description of a place of perfect tranquility and rest for those who die before the coming resurrection. It is a sea spread out beneath and before the throne of God. Although connected to the throne room of God, where there are roarings, thunderings and worshipful commotions, it is a separate place in the third heaven, yet it is in the presence of God (II Cor. 5:8). The tranquility of this sea is represented in its calm, smooth surface, hence, a Sea of Glass.

Contrary to fanciful belief, those who die in the Lord are not seen in Scripture as praising God, jumping, running and enjoying a mansion. Not yet. They are at rest, at peace, awaiting the resurrection. They do not have their glorified bodies yet. They do not receive their new bodies until the resurrection. At that time, the awakened souls will be reunited with their bodies. Then the corruptible and immortal body will put on incorruption and immortality (I Cor. 15:51–55). The soul will remain at rest until its reunion with the body. I believe that the soul is aware of the most blissful rest and peace imaginable, but it is at rest, asleep in Jesus (I Thess. 4:14–15). This Sea of Glass will be emptied when the Rapture of the Church takes place, only to be used again for the martyrs of the Tribulation Period (mingled with fire — Rev. 15:2).

To whatever degree, the soul at rest is aware of the most perfect peace and contentment imaginable. As it is with earthly sleep, the individual's soul is unaware of the passage of time. Time is irrelevant.

The Awakening

Sleep and rest necessitates an awakening, which

will occur at the Rapture (I Thess. 4:16). It is in this rest that the apostles and all of the other saints who have died from the Day of Pentecost to this present day are contently awaiting the resurrection. If you or I should die today, and the Rapture occurs ten, twenty or thirty years from now, the passage of time would be as nothing. It is a place where time, as we know it, does not exist. It would be as if we simply went to sleep and were awakened by the trump of God to be caught up with Christ.

As seen earlier, the Sea of Glass is the destination for the Christian at death. It is the "rest" between death and the resurrection.

> "There remaineth therefore a rest to the people of God. For he that is entered into his rest, he also hath ceased from his own works, as God did from his. Let us labour therefore to enter into that rest, lest any man fall after the same example of unbelief" (Hebrews 4:9–11).

What About the Rapture?

Those of us who are alive at the resurrection will not sleep. Paul calls this a mystery:

> "Behold, I shew you a mystery; We shall not all sleep, but we shall all be changed, In a moment, in the twinkling of an eye, at the last trump: for the trumpet shall sound, and the dead shall be raised incorruptible, and we shall be changed" (I Corinthians 15:51–52).

> "For if we believe that Jesus died and rose again, even so them also which sleep in Jesus will God bring with him. For

this we say unto you by the word of the Lord, that we which are alive and remain unto the coming of the Lord shall not prevent them which are asleep" (I Thessalonians 4:14–15).

Soul Sleep

The believer's rest is not to be confused with the theory of "Soul Sleep." Soul Sleep, as held by many, denies a conscious existence between death and the resurrection based upon the condition of the body. As discussed earlier, the body does indeed cease to function as a breathing, thinking organism at death. However, according to the Soul Sleep theory, the soul is a combination of body and soul. When the body dies, so does the soul. Therefore, both body and soul lay dead in the grave. This theory has some major flaws. If Soul Sleep were true, nothing is actually left to enjoy a rest, for the soul ceases to exist. This also denies the Scripture that says to be absent from the body is to be present with the Lord (II Cor. 5:8) and we know that the Lord is not in the grave. What then is called a resurrection to those adhering to Soul Sleep would actually be a re-creation. The Soul Sleep theory is completely unscriptural. *A-men!*

Those who die in the Lord during the present age will remain in their "rest" until the Rapture of the Church. It is more than a mere spiritual aberration. Considering what we have found in our study thus far, death for the Christian would be as though one went to sleep, was aware of the most perfect rest imaginable, and will be awakened to experience the resurrection.

Another Destination: Old Testament Paradise

When Jesus arose from the dead, He changed the destination of Old Testament saints. Before the cross of Calvary, it was impossible for the souls of the righteous to enter into God's presence in the third heaven. At this time they could not enter into the Sea of Glass to await the resurrection. Their rest was not there, but in another place of peace and contentment.

The Old Testament saints worshiped God under the Law of Moses by sacrificing bulls, goats and other animals, along with various other operations. These sacrifices were only forerunners of the ultimate sacrifice for sin, Jesus Christ. The blood of bulls and goats could not take away man's sins; it could only cover them.

> "But in those sacrifices there is a remembrance again made of sins every year. For it is not possible that the blood of bulls and of goats should take away sins" (Hebrews 10:3–4).

The Old Testament saints could not enter into the presence of the one holy God in heaven until the perfect sacrifice for sin was made. That perfect sacrifice was Jesus.

The destination of Old Testament saints prior to the cross was a place called paradise. For Old Testament saints, paradise was synonymous with "Abraham's bosom." To these saints death meant "to be with their fathers" (Gen. 15:15; 47:30; Deut. 31:16; Jdg. 2:10; Lk. 3:8; Jn. 8:37–40). Reference to Abraham's bosom was considered a place of rest, a secure place after death. It was paradise, a destination for the faithful dead (Lk. 16:22). Where was this paradise?

Lower Parts?

We are told that between the crucifixion and the resurrection, Christ went into the lower parts of the Earth. These lower parts were two compartments of a place called *sheowl* (Hebrew for Hades).

> "Wherefore he saith, When he ascended up on high, he led captivity captive, and gave gifts unto men. (Now that he ascended, what is it but that he also descended first into the lower parts of the earth? He that descended is the same also that ascended up far above all heavens, that he might fill all things)" (Ephesians 4:8–10).

The lower parts (plural) of the Earth not only included Hades (Gk. of *sheowl*), the prison for the disobedient, but also included a paradise. Note that this was before the resurrection of Christ. Thus, one part was that of torment and the other part was a paradise. There was a great gulf separating the two. We see this in the narrative of the rich man and Lazarus (Lk. 16:26). It was to the side of paradise that Jesus took the thief on the cross.

> "And he said unto Jesus, Lord, remember me when thou comest into thy kingdom. And Jesus said unto him, Verily I

say unto thee, To day shalt thou be with me **in paradise**" (Luke 23:42–43).

Christ did not arise until three days later, yet He told the thief on the cross that "...to day shalt thou be with me in paradise." We have already seen that Jesus descended into the lower parts of the Earth before ascending into heaven. This reveals that paradise was included in the lower parts of the Earth at the time of the crucifixion.

King Saul's impatient act recorded in I Samuel also reveals that paradise was in the lower parts of the Earth. The Philistines had come to wage war against Israel. King Saul inquired of the Lord about the matter, but the Lord didn't answer. In an act of impatience, Saul went to the witch of Endor to make his inquiry. He wanted her to bring up Samuel from the dead.

Samuel's spirit did arise, but this was evidently a work of the Lord because it scared the witch terribly. She apparently wasn't accustomed to seeing such a thing. She cried, "I saw gods ascending out of the earth." The point is that Samuel was disquieted from within the Earth. He said to Saul, "Why hast thou disquieted me, **to bring me up**" (I Sam. 28:11–15). Note that Samuel was quieted and became disquieted. He was in his rest in paradise.

Captivity Captive

Christ led captivity captive (Eph. 4:8) when He rose from the dead. That is, those who were in paradise were taken out and transported to the Sea of Glass directly beneath and before the throne of God (Rev. 4:6). Samuel was in that crowd also. This was when Christ moved paradise from within the Earth to the Sea of Glass in heaven. He led those captive in paradise (within the Earth) to captivity in heaven (the Sea of Glass), thus, leading "captivity captive." This was not a cruel captivity, but a secure place of rest and peace. This part within the Earth called paradise, now emptied, would be overtaken by the torturous side, for hell continues to enlarge itself as it had begun to do in Isaiah's day (Isa. 5:14).

Again, the Old Testament saints could not enter into God's presence because the ultimate sacrifice for sin had not been made until Christ' death, burial, and resurrection. Therefore, we recognize another destination for Old Testament saints called "paradise" that existed before the cross. The Old Testament saints are currently in the place of perfect peace and tranquility in the Sea of Glass awaiting the resurrection as we await the resurrection.

The Apostle Peter also mentioned the descent of Christ into the lower parts of the Earth:

> "For Christ also hath once suffered for sins, the just for the unjust, that he might bring us to God, being put to death in the flesh, but quickened by the Spirit: By which also he went and preached unto the spirits in prison; Which sometime were disobedient, when once the longsuffering of God waited in the days of Noah, while the ark was a preparing,

wherein few, that is, eight souls were saved by water" (I Peter 3:18–20).

In the time between the crucifixion and the resurrection, Christ descended into Hades (Gk. for "hell"), which is located within the Earth's core (see also Acts 2:24–27). Not only did He lead captivity captive but He also preached to the "spirits in prison." Many contend that the recipients of this message were those who were alive before the Flood of Noah and that Christ, by the Spirit, traveled to Noah's day and preached to them. However, the reference above concerns the time immediately following Christ's death on the cross. It is then that the sin that Jesus became on behalf of mankind was delivered to its place (II Cor. 5:21). Then our Savior could arise with a glorified body. In Hades Noah's faith and example were vindicated before the spirits in prison. Christ did not go there to give those spirits a second chance, but to proclaim His triumph and vindicate the way of faith, the victorious faith, that Noah had held before them.

Enter the Transition

We have seen that those who die in the Lord during this present dispensation will be resurrected at the trump of God (I Thess. 4:13–18). Those born-again believers who are still alive when the resurrection occurs will be caught up together with the dead in Christ. We will experience the Judgment Seat of Christ (I Cor. 3:11–15) and the Marriage Supper of the Lamb

(Rev. 19:7–9), and will return with our Lord at the Second Coming (Zech. 14:5; Col. 3:4; I Thess. 3:13; Jude 14). We will witness victory at the Battle of Armegeddon (Rev. 19:17–19) and the judgment of nations (Matt. 25:31–46), and prepare for the destination of Authority.

The Destination of Authority

We discussed God's overall plan in Chapter Four. We found that we are to rule and reign with Christ during what is termed the "Millennial Reign."

One must wonder why there should be a Millennial Reign or Millennial Kingdom at all. Why not just wipe out everything and begin the new heaven and new Earth? The most significant reason is that Scripture must be fulfilled. When God makes a promise, He keeps it. Note that God created the Earth and set it up for man to have dominion. God gave Adam dominion and Adam lost it to Satan. The Earth will be redeemed by its Owner and Creator when Jesus returns (Col. 1:12–17). He will then rule the Earth and bring the righteousness to it that was intended — the righteousness that man could not bring about himself. The Second Coming is not only for our redemption, but also for the redemption of Earth's dominion. In addition, the kingdom reign is necessary to fulfill Scripture (Lk. 1:32). It is then that Christ will rule on David's throne, an earthly throne specifically designed for an earthly rule.

Many will survive the terrible Tribulation Period that occurs after the Rapture of the Church. Those who are considered the "sheep" nations in Matthew 25:31–46 will live during the Millennial Reign. They will not reign as "joint heirs," nor will they possess glorified bodies. They will live in their natural bodies during that time. Those of us who will have been raptured will have glorified bodies and rule and reign with Christ (Rom. 8:17). We will have received our glorified bodies at the Rapture.

What a wonderful time for those of us who will enter into that time of peace. It will be a secure place with all the pleasures of the kingdom at our fingertips. There will be no evil actions of nation against nation (Zeph. 3:13–15). Even the animals will be at peace (Hos. 2:18). The wolf will lie down with the lamb. The cow and the bear will feed together. The child will place his hand in the den of a venomous snake and will not be harmed:

> "The wolf also shall dwell with the lamb, and the leopard shall lie down with the kid; and the calf and the young lion and the fatling together; and a little child shall lead them. And the cow and the bear shall feed; their young ones shall lie down together: and the lion shall eat straw like the ox. And the sucking child shall play on the hole of the asp, and the weaned child shall put his hand on the cockatrice' den. They shall not hurt nor destroy in all my holy mountain: for the earth shall be full of the knowledge of the LORD, as the waters cover the sea" (Isaiah 11:6–9).

The Millennial Reign is the period that even the animals have travailed for (Rom. 8:19–22). During that time all animals will be tame. What a beautiful thing to witness! To be with Christ as "joint heirs" and to rule and reign with Him has to be one of the most joyous and wondrous things imaginable for the Church and those martyred for Christ during the Tribulation Period (Rev. 3:21). In addition, it will be a wondrous place to live for those who will go into that time in their physical bodies (those surviving the Tribulation Period and judgment of the nations).

Pets in Heaven

Many wonder whether pets go to heaven. As we saw in Chapter Two, animals were not created in the image and likeness of God. They do not possess the reasoning and compassionate qualities of man. Many animals are very intelligent; however, they learn only by what God has supplied in nature and by human tutoring. They contain souls only in the meaning of physical life (Eccl. 3:18–20). To have an eternal soul with the ability to reason and make intelligent choices would subject pets to accepting or rejecting salvation along with the plight of heaven or hell. This is not the case. Animals cannot reason in this fashion because they were not created that way. Although there will undoubtedly be animals during the Millennial Reign and on the new Earth, they do not contain a three-fold nature as does man. They are subject to restoration as seen above, but not individually to eternal life. When they die they return to dust and exist no more. Only through the next generation of offspring do they have a semblance of on-going life.

> "All go unto one place; all are of the dust, and all turn to dust again. Who knoweth the spirit of man that goeth upward, and the spirit of the beast that goeth downward to the earth?" (Ecclesiastes 3:20–21).

The Eternal Destination

> "And I saw a new heaven and a new earth: for the first heaven and the first earth were passed away; and there was no more sea. And I John saw the holy city, new Jerusalem, coming down from God out of heaven, prepared as a bride adorned for her husband" (Revelation 21:1–2).

Here we view the new status of God's ancient works of art: the heaven and the Earth. The new heaven and the new Earth are the results of the purification of the atmospheric heaven and the Earth by fire (II Peter 3:10). In the previous chapter we read the words "passed away" from *parerchomai,* which means to "change from one condition to another." This is exactly what will happen to the Earth and its atmospheric heaven. The term *parerchomai* is also used to verify the status of the unchangeable Word (Matt. 24:35; Mrk. 13:31; Lk. 21:33).

John doesn't see a sea on the new Earth, because the prophesied fiery judgment will lap up all of the waters. The absence of the sea does not mean that there will be no more water at all, for water will once again flow in abundance on the new Earth from the river that flows out from God's throne (Rev. 22:1–2).

A New Eternal City

In addition to the new heaven and new Earth, John also sees the holy city, New Jerusalem, coming down from God out of heaven. Note that it is the city, not the Earth, that descends. The new Earth, on which the new city sits, shall be, and indeed already is, in place. To us it will be a city; to the Father, it is a house. It takes many houses to constitute a community, township or city. Likewise, the many mansions of the Father's house will constitute a city. The name of this city is the New Jerusalem, the "place" that Jesus has gone away to prepare (Jn. 14:1–7). It is the Father's *oikia,* His residence, His abode, His house of many mansions. Lyrics to an old familiar hymn read, "Just build me a cabin in the corner of glory land." These are humble words, but they are unscriptural. Nobody will get a log cabin. We will get many mansions in a brand new city constructed from the most elaborate of materials.

The materials used for this new city are not mere wood, brick or mortar, but they are the best of the best. The walls are made of jasper and the streets are made of pure gold. It is a very real and literal place. These walls and streets are not ethereal or spiritual aberrations of the mind; they are real, tangible properties to be felt and enjoyed. We call this place heaven, because it will be heavenly. God calls it the New Jerusalem.

God Dwells With Man

> "And I heard a great voice out of heaven saying, Behold, the tabernacle of God is with men, and he will dwell with them, and they shall be his people, and God himself shall be with them, and be their God. And God shall wipe away all tears from their eyes; and there shall be no more death, neither sorrow, nor crying, neither shall there be any more pain: for the former things are passed away" (Revelation 21:3–4).

Note that we will not go to dwell where God dwells; that is, we will not dwell in the third heaven or paradise, into which Paul and John were caught up. The key word here is "dwell." It is God who comes to dwell with man on a perfectly purified Earth in a brand new city. It's God's tabernacle that is to be with men.

The word "tabernacle" comes from the Greek word *skene,* which means "a tent or cloth hut." This denotes a temporary dwelling; however, *skene* also means "habitation." God will not take up temporary residence but He will "dwell" with men. The new city will be His habitation. Out of all the celestial bodies in the universe, God has chosen to dwell upon this beautiful planet called Earth. It will be purified by fire and will flourish once again for that habitation (II Peter 3:10; Psa. 78:69).

The tabernacle of old was a symbol of God's protection and communion with man. We will enjoy this protection and communion in the new city on the newly purified Earth. We will reside with God and continually commune with Him. It is the time in which the Father, the Word, and the Holy Spirit will be all in all (I Cor. 15:28). There will be no tears, no death, no crying and no pain.

Perfect Security

Not only will we have direct communion with God, but we will have the security of His omnipotence. He is all powerful; He is the Almighty. Nothing will be threatening. Such total and complete security is incomprehensible in our present state. We can only imagine what this kind of security will be like. We will experience all the bliss of perfect security in the presence of God Almighty. It will be awesome!

Only through faith are we able to accept that such a world will exist, and that God's words are true and are faithful (Heb. 11:6). Our faith is a wonderful blessing, for through faith our spirit bears witness with God's Spirit that the Word of God is sure! (Rom. 8:16–17).

The Glory of the City

John sees the New Jerusalem in Revelation 21:2. This city is not a place made up of mere man-made buildings, businesses and parks; it is a glorious city adorned as a bride. Although it is full of mansions, it takes occupants to make a city. The occupants of the new city are those who make up the Bride, born-again believers in Christ Jesus from the Church Age (II Cor. 11:2). Thus, John sees both the city and the occupants in the form of God's "glory." Why? Because the New Jerusalem is also our glory as the Bride of Christ. We know this, for we are joint-heirs with Jesus Christ and He is God (Jn. 1:1–14). We will be with Him forever (I Thess. 4:17) and He will dwell in the new city (Rev. 21: 3–4, 23). John saw the glory of God, the glory of the wife (Bride becomes the wife), and the glory of the city combined as one unit in his vision. The Bride will become the wife (at the Marriage Supper of the Lamb) and the city are inseparable references in the book of Revelation.

Thus, alongside the glory of the Lamb, we, too, will light up the city. The wife lights up the city? How? The glory of God has mainly been shown in Christ in the New Testament (Lk. 9:29–32; Jn. 2:11). As joint-heirs, believers also share in that glory (Jn. 17:5–6, 22). Thus, we are to be transformed into the "glorious" image of God (II Cor. 3:18). We are now made in the image of God, but then the glorious image and we will be fully glorified when in His presence (Rom. 5:2). John saw a combination of both the city and the wife as having the glory of God. The brightness of God's glory is the primary reason that John sees the city instead of a woman. The brightness of God's glory, as witnessed by Paul, will outshine even the midday sun (Acts 26:13).

The Size of the City

> "And he that talked with me had a golden reed to measure the city, and the gates thereof, and the wall thereof. And the city lieth foursquare, and the length is as large as the breadth: and he measured the city with the reed, twelve thousand furlongs. The length and the breadth and the height of it are equal. And he measured the wall thereof, an hundred and forty and four cubits, according to the measure of a man, that is, of the angel. And the building of the wall of it was of jasper: and the city was pure gold, like unto clear glass" (Revelation 21:15–18).

It would be fitting for us to have some idea of the place where we will spend eternity. Therefore, God has given us a description of our new home. And what a home it will be!

The angel had a golden reed with which to measure the city, the gates and the wall. The city measures 12,000 furlongs, 1,500 miles long and 1,500 miles wide. Such a city would extend from Maine to Florida and from the East Coast to about 600 miles west of the Mississippi River. (The U.S. is only being used as a reference).

Foursquare City

Note that the city lies foursquare or *tetragonos,* which means being four-cornered. The length is as large as the breadth. The singular form of the word "wall" is used here. Although viewing the city will give the appearance of having four walls, it will be one continual wall surrounding the city not having any breaks or joints. This wall will have twelve openings because there are twelve gates to the city. It is unblemished and seamless: a perfect wall for a perfect city.

It would seem reasonable that this great wall is shaped like a mountain peak rather than a cube. Note that it "lieth" or "sits" foursquare or "four-cornered," not upward in the shape of a cube having eight corners. Scripture does not say whether the top of the city is canopied or open. However, a mountain peak shape would appear to have better supporting qualities for a literal city. The main reason for this assumption is that the wall is only 216 feet thick (144 cubits). This would be a relatively thin wall for a cubical shape and would be completely out of proportion. A pyramidal shape with such a wall would be self-supporting: remember that the wall extends 1,500 miles in length and in width. Another reason is that the throne of God will evidently be positioned in the center of the city and upward because the river of life originates and flows from "out of the throne."

Wall of Jasper

The structure of the wall is made of jasper, a variety of quartz or silicon dioxide. Silicon, which constitutes more than one-fourth of the Earth's crust, is used in making steel. Although the wall is crystal clear, it will be as strong, if not stronger, than steel. The wall is of jasper but the city — including the streets — is made of pure gold, which is crystal clear. (The impurities in gold give it the yellowish color we see today). This city is constructed without the use of human hands; its builder and maker is God (Heb. 11:10). This is the place Jesus (God in the flesh) went away to prepare (Jn. 14:2–3). A beautiful song describes this wonderful place: "Oh, What a City." We will surely have to see it to even imagine its glory because this place is truly beyond description.

What Shall Be Our Likeness?

"Beloved, now are we the sons of God, and it doth not yet appear what we shall be: but we know that, when he shall appear, we shall be like him; for we shall see him as he is" (I John 3:2).

We could stop at this verse and dismiss any questions; however, we have all been curious at one time or another about what *we* will be like. The Apostle John said that it was not yet manifested what we would be like after the resurrection. Even the most intelligent and greatest theologians can only guess what we will be like. But John gives us a hint by saying that we will be like Christ. Although we cannot presently comprehend the fullness of Christ, we can glean an idea of our coming glorified nature from the scriptural descriptions of Christ after His resurrection.

"...Ye men of Galilee, why stand ye gazing up into heaven? **this same Jesus,** which is taken up from you into heaven, shall so come in like manner as ye have seen him go into heaven" (Acts 1:11).

Not only will Jesus return in the same manner as He left, but He will be the "same" Jesus. In previous verses we have seen that when Jesus returns at the Second Coming we will be with Him (Zech 14:5; Col. 3:4; I Thess. 3:13; Jude 14). John said that when He appears we will be like Him; therefore, at least a portion of our eternal make-up will involve the possession of a glorified body like the body Jesus had when He ascended, and the one with which He will evidently return. To be glorified means more than position and reward; it means that we will have a changed nature and existence. As seen earlier, we will possess the glory of God. This glorified nature refers only to those raptured saints who are now called the Bride of Christ (II Cor. 11:2), and who will become the wife (Rev. 19:7–9); that is, we will have an eternal, glorified relationship.

When Jesus appeared to the disciples after the resurrection, He had a body of flesh and bone — a testimony to His literal and physical resurrection. His resurrection was not merely an ethereal or spiritual resurrection. Therefore it is evident that we, too, will possess glorified bodies of flesh and bone. They will be tangible, flesh-and-bone bodies that can be touched

(Lk. 24:39). We will be able to eat and drink (Matt. 26:29; Mrk. 14:25; Lk. 24:42).

Bone – Blood

Here we must consider that flesh and blood cannot inherit the kingdom of God (I Cor. 15:50). Is there a contradiction? No. Although this is a direct reference to our mortal bodies, which decay and die, it also states a fact about the kingdom of God: we must become immortal in order to participate in the eternal kingdom. First Corinthians 15:50 does not necessarily mean that flesh and *bone* cannot inherit the kingdom of God, especially glorified flesh and *bone*. It does mean that flesh and *blood,* an integral part of the life-flow of mortal man, cannot inherit the kingdom of God.

It becomes apparent that the combination of flesh with blood constitutes a great difference from flesh and bone. Blood was used as a sin atonement (Matt. 26:28; Mrk. 14:24; Acts 20:28; Rom. 3:25; 5:9; Eph. 1:7; Col. 1:14; Heb. 9:7,12–14,22; 13:11–12; I Jn. 1:7; Rev. 1:5). No sin in heaven will be atoned for, so there will be no need for blood. We must also note that blood was used many times as a curse (Matt. 9:20; 23:30; 23:35; 27:4,6,8,25; Lk. 11:50; Acts 2:19; 5:28; 18:6). There will be no more curse in heaven; there-fore, those who possess a glorified body will have no use for blood. Moreover, Jesus shed His blood. To shed something means to get rid of it completely.

Clearly, our resurrected and glorified bodies will be bloodless. This seems impossible to comprehend because blood carries oxygen, the breath of life. This is not impossible for glorified man because we will have a changed nature.

We know that Jesus' death was the avenue by which man may obtain eternal life (I Thess. 4:14). This necessitated the shedding of blood. Jesus did not mention flesh and blood when He appeared to the disciples, for the blood had been shed on the cross so that immortality might reign. Note, it is not the blood in and of itself that cleanses, but also its shedding:

"And almost all things are by the law purged with blood; and without shedding of blood is no remission" (Hebrews 9:22).

Behold My Hands and My Feet

Our new bodies will possess supernatural abilities. Jesus disappeared from sight when He ascended into heaven. After ministering to the two men on the Emmaus road, Jesus "vanished" from their sight (Lk. 24:31). Also, it seems as though Jesus could appear and disappear at will in Luke 24:37. When Jesus appeared to the disciples, they were locked behind a "shut" door because they feared the Jews. This door was more than just closed. It was securely shut. When the disciples saw Him, they were terrified; they thought they were seeing a ghost (evidently appearing before them, and bloodless). Jesus immediately comforted their troubled spirits. He replied:

> "...Why are ye troubled? and why do thoughts arise in your hearts? Behold my hands and my feet, that it is I myself: handle me, and see; for a spirit hath not flesh and bones, as ye see me have" (Luke 24:38–39).

As the Angels in Heaven

The Sadducees were members of a religious sect who refused to believe in the resurrection of the body. They often questioned Jesus and tried to discredit Him by trickery. The Sadducees knew of a childless man who had a wife and seven brothers. This man died. It was lawful for a brother to marry a widow in order to continue the "seed of the brother." The Sadducees challenged Jesus with this hypothetical situation: the childless man died, and each of the seven brothers married this woman. Each of them died without having children with her. They asked Jesus, "Therefore in the resurrection whose wife shall she be of the seven? for they all had her" (Matt. 22:28).

Their reasoning was apparent: If Jesus couldn't answer this question, then it was certain there was no resurrection. However, Jesus rebuked them for their ignorance of the Scriptures and their ignorance of the power of God. He said, "Ye do err" (Matt. 22:29). Jesus then commented on one aspect of those resurrected. He said, "For in the resurrection they neither marry, nor are given in marriage, but are as the angels of God in heaven" (Matt. 22:30).

We must keep in mind that Christians will have been born into another family beyond the bounds of human condition and procreation. We are all brothers and sisters in the Lord (Gal. 3:28); we are a family. However, Jesus stated that there aren't any marriages or marriage arrangements in the resurrection. This does not discount the fact that such relationships are not carried over by knowledge into the world to come, for we will undoubtedly know one another. In addition, this concerns one-on-one relationships, for after the resurrection comes the Marriage Supper of the Lamb.

If, indeed, earthly relationships are carried over into the glorified state, they will be without human vice. In other words, jealousy, discord, envy, strife and all other sinful characteristics will be gone. Procreation will cease and we will live in heaven as do the angels.

Yet another question is this: Will we know our family members as we did on Earth? What about those we knew who died without Christ? The answer lies in birth: We do not know those who were never born into our natural families. As far as we are concerned, they never existed (except in cases of miscarriage, abortion, etc.). The same will be true of those who are never born into the family of God. To those who are in their glorified state, it will be as though the unsaved never existed. Revelation 21 explains that there will be no tears in heaven. That means there will be no sorrow or pain. It would be devastating for a wife whose husband or children do not go to heaven. But in that place where marriage is irrelevant, she will never have known them, because they will not have been born into the family of God. Likewise, marriage will not be an issue because, like the angels, we will not marry (Matt. 22:30).

To Know As We Are Known?

Doesn't Scripture say that we shall know even as we are known?

> "For now we see through a glass, darkly; but then face to face: now I know in part; but then shall I know even as also I am known" (I Corinthians 13:12).

Although I believe that we will know one another in the Lord, the above verse is not a direct reference to our knowledge of our earthly positions as mothers, fathers, and so on. It is an assurance that we will know Christ as He now knows us. No one knows us the way Jesus Christ does. He knows us better than we even know ourselves. The veil of darkness will be lifted when we receive our glorified bodies and we will know Christ in His fullness as He knows us.

Will They Know Me?

Will we know our earthly spouses, fathers, mothers, sons or daughters? Yes, I believe we will.

Scripture is not void concerning our knowing one another after the resurrection. Each person will be judged and rewarded according to his or her own works (I Cor. 3:12–15): that's individuality. Some will suffer loss of reward, but he "himself" will be saved (v.15). That, too, is individuality. King David, who had lost his son, evidently believed that he would know his son after death. He said,

> "But now he is dead, wherefore should I fast? can I bring him back again? I shall go to him, but he shall not return to me" (II Samuel 12:23).

Is it reasonable to believe, then, that we will retain somewhat of an earthly identity? I believe so, because we will possess flesh and bone. As I mentioned earlier, this existence will be without any trace of human vice. We only see through a glass darkly right now, but one day we will see Christ face to face and will have perfect knowledge. This knowledge will include earthly relationships in the Lord, but will far exceed anything we are able to imagine (Pro. 24:3–4; Eph. 3:20). We will know exactly what it means to be "in Christ," where there is neither male nor female:

> "There is neither Jew nor Greek, there is neither bond nor free, there is neither male nor female: for ye are all one in Christ Jesus" (Galatians 3:28).

Perfect knowledge will allow us to know each individual as Christ knows each of us. I will know Christ completely and all who are His. I will also be known by every other individual because we will all have such knowledge. In heaven, the true meaning of family and the fatherhood of God will hit us like a ton of bricks.

I believe that God has a plan for us that far exceeds any conceivable idea or ritual that man can imagine. It will be so far beyond carnal attachments and boundaries that the former things will be completely irrelevant (Rev. 21:4). Ω

CHAPTER
6

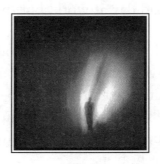

DESTINATIONS
PART 2: HELL

Hell is becoming an outdated destination by today's thinking, but it is certainly not out of business.

This chapter deals with hell, an unpopular and greatly avoided aspect of God's plan. To many, hell is nothing more than a curse or expression of contempt; to others, hell is but the strife of daily living. Hell may even be compared to a family situation or a bad day at work, but that's man's hell, not God's hell.

The same all-wise, all-knowing God who designed and created heaven also designed and created hell. All things were created by Him (Col. 1:16–17). God's hell is a literal place with physical consequences for those who end up there. It was created for all who are deemed unfit for heaven.

Hell was not prepared for humans, but for the devil and his angels (Matt. 25:41). However, all those who have died without accepting God's plan of escape, by the very nature of rejection, have accepted the devil's plight and plan (I Jn. 3:8). Such people are referred to in Scripture as the "children of disobedience" (Eph. 5:6). These people have the devil's spirit; they are even called the devil's children (Jn. 8:42–45). God's wrath will be their inheritance, because they are the children of wrath (Eph. 2:2–3; 5:6; I Jn. 3:10). But praise be to God that there is a way of escape for all who will accept it (Rom. 3:23; 6:23; 5:8; 10:9).

Sadly, hell is a subject that many of today's theologians do not take very seriously. It has become out of step with the thinking of modern society: Many contend that it is difficult enough to defend Christianity without having to explain hell. But, like it or not, hell is more than a theological discomfort; it is a reality. Most assuredly, Jesus portrayed hell that way. It was more than a scare tactic or spooky phenomenon used by Jesus in His ministry. So if Jesus took hell seriously, so should we. It is our duty to learn all we can about hell and the plight of those who go there.

The Destination of Hell

The word "hell" is translated in the King James Bible from three Greek words in the New Testament and one Hebrew word in the Old Testament. The Greek words are: *haides* (hades), *geena* (gehenna), and *tartaroo* (tartaros). The original Old Testament Hebrew word for "hell" is *sheowl*. *Sheowl* or *Sheol* has a double application that is sometimes used to designate the grave and other times to refer to the place of departed spirits.

In reality, the hells of both Old and New Testaments are different stages and/or divisions of the one place of torment. The stages and divisions are explained as follows:

1. *Hades*. This is the same as the Old Testament word *sheowl*, the place where we find those of both Old and New Testaments who have died (and are dying) without accepting God's plan of escape. We discussed the two compartments of Hades in the

previous chapter, however, Hades does not presently include the paradise side because Christ emptied paradise when He led captivity captive (Psa. 68:18; Eph. 4:8). Those who die without having accepted Christ, in addition to the disobedient of Old Testament times, are held in Hades until the Great White Throne Judgment takes place (Rev. 20:12). We know that Hades is a place of torment as described in Luke 16:19–31. As mentioned earlier, Jesus descended into Hades before He ascended into heaven (Acts 2:24–27; Eph. 4:8–10; I Peter 3:18–20).

2. *Tartaros.* *Tartaros* is from the Greek *tartaroo* and is found in II Peter 2:4. *Tartaros* is the lowest abyss of Hades. Both Peter and Jude inform us that this is where the fallen angels are being kept. These fallen angels are those of the spirit-world who were cast out with Satan (Rev. 12:4; Jude 6). They are evidently locked in this abyss and are restrained from roaming the higher elevation of Hades. *Tartaros*, this lowest abyss of hell, is the bottomless pit. It is called the "bottomless pit" simply because it has no bottom. If one could do so, one could descend to the very center of the Earth, but would merely have to stop, because there is no bottom. To continue to move in any direction, one would immediately begin to ascend (as the Earth is round).

The very word "bottomless" gives reference to the downward direction of this place. The demons besought Christ not to cast them into the deep when Christ met the man at Gadarene (Lk. 8:26–36). This "deep" is *abussos,* which is "abyss (bottomless) pit."

Note: These beings of Luke 8:26–36 were not cast into the abyss when the fallen angels were cast there after their expulsion with Satan (then called Lucifer). These demonic creatures were the spirit-flesh beings, or offspring, of the sons of God (angels as sons — Job 1:6; 2:1) and the daughters of men (Gen. 6:2–5). The offspring of this union are referred to as the Nephilim, from the Hebrew word *nephiyl,* meaning "giant" (Gen. 6:4). These beings were part human, part fallen angel. This is where such legends as half-god, half-human heroes were born, including Hercules and many others. When these offspring physically died, the fallen angel spirit within lived on (for spirits cannot die, Gen. 6:3). Hence, these beings (demons) became disembodied spirits. These disembodied spirits are ever searching for new bodies to inhabit. They do not die when the bodies of their victims die. This is why so many people are drawn to the occult through psychics, mediums, familiar spirits and a belief in reincarnation. Upon opening themselves up to the occult, that is, the world of "familiar" spirits, they become possessed, or at least persuaded, by these immortal beings who have lived in previous bodies. The re-embodied spirit, having the thoughts and memories of previous victims, conveys those thoughts and memories to the new victim. The new victim is convinced that he or she has lived a previous life. This is one of Satan's many deceptive tactics.

3. *Geenna* or *Gehenna,* the everlasting hell, will be the eternal abode of the "dead" who are judged at the Great White Throne Judgment (Matt. 5:22; 23:33; Rev. 20:11–15). It will also be the eternal dwelling place of Satan and all other fallen angels (Matt. 25:41; Rev. 20:10), and all humans who have rejected God's plan of escape (Heb. 2:3). The Great White Throne Judgment does not occur until after the Millennial Reign; this eternal stage of hell has not yet begun. Its eternal nature will begin when the beast and the false prophet of Revelation 19:20 are cast there (see author's book, *The Unveiling*). *Geenna* (*gehenna*) is the "lake of fire" of Scripture (Rev. 19:20; 20:10,14,15) which is the second death (Rev. 20:14). *Gehenna* as a garbage dump will be discussed in pages forthcoming.

Does God Send Anyone to Hell?
It has been said that the belief in hell has driven

many people away from Christianity. Such people will have nothing to do with a loving God who would send someone to a tormentous hell. It doesn't seem like the punishment fits the crime — it's like getting the death penalty for speeding!

God doesn't send anyone to hell. He loves people so much that He made a way of escape from hell for everyone who will accept it (Jn. 3:16). People go to hell because they choose to go. It is certain that God will pass judgment upon sin; however, every individual who is capable of thought has been given the choice to accept or reject God's plan of escape.

All sin must be delivered to its proper place because it is unfit for heaven. Therefore, if someone has chosen to reject God's plan of escape through Christ and dies, that person's choice of sin, not God, has condemned his soul (Jn. 3:17).

> "For God sent not his Son into the world to condemn the world; but that the world through him might be saved. He that believeth on him is not condemned: but he that believeth not is condemned already, because he hath not believed in the name of the only begotten Son of God" (John 3:17–18).

One who denies Christ incurs God's wrath, which is to fall upon the devil, his angels, and the devil's children (Eph. 2:2–3; I Jn 3:10). The Holy Spirit convicts men to accept God's plan (Jn. 6:44). To openly deny the call is to speak against the Holy Ghost (Spirit). The unpardonable sin is to remain in disbelief. This sin will not be forgiven in this world or in the world to come (Matt. 12:32).

God extends the call of salvation to everyone. That call rings out throughout the lives of every individual (Acts 17:30; Rom. 11:29); however, God "...will by no means clear the guilty" without repentance (Ex. 34:7). Accepting Christ as personal Savior is the most important decision one can possibly make (Jn. 14:6).

Matthew and Luke's Gospel accounts contain Jesus' warnings that God is to be feared more than the most powerful of men. Men can only kill the body; but God is able to cast one into hell and destroy both body and soul.

> "And fear not them which kill the body, but are not able to kill the soul: but rather fear him which is able to destroy both soul and body in hell" (Matthew 10:28).

> "And I say unto you my friends, Be not afraid of them that kill the body, and after that have no more that they can do. But I will forewarn you whom ye shall fear: Fear him, which after he hath killed hath power to cast into hell; yea, I say unto you, Fear him" (Luke 12:4–5).

The word "destroy" comes from the Greek word *apollumi*. It does not mean to annihilate. The idea is not extinction but ruin. It is the loss of well being, not the loss of being (*Vine's Expository Dictionary Of New Testament Words*).

Apollumi is also used in passages such as Matthew 9:17; Luke 15:4; and John 6:12,27. In none of these instances does it mean to pass out of existence, or to annihilate. Therefore, to "destroy" means to bring to an everlasting state of ruin. An individual who has chosen hell will not deteriorate to annihilation. His eternal soul will be joined to an indestructible resurrected body (resurrected for the Great White Throne Judgment and Gehenna hell — Dan. 12:2; Rev. 20:12).

Death is an appointment made by God (Heb. 9:27); therefore, we must take Christ's warning to heart, because hell is serious business (Rom. 6:22–23).

The Eternity of Hell

Is hell really eternal? A good example of liberal reasoning concerning this subject is found in the Roman Catholic teaching of "Purgatory." The concept of Purgatory, or the temporal punishment for mortal sins, was not invented until approximately one thousand years after Christ's death. It is purely a Roman Catholic doctrine and is completely unscriptural. The sale of indulgences was also invented to offset the punishment received in Purgatory. An indulgence can consist of works or a financial payment. According to the theory, enough money can spring a soul from Hades. If this sounds fishy, that's because it is. Peter said, "Thy money perish with thee, because thou hast thought that the gift of God may be purchased with money" (Acts 8:20). (See author's book, *The Unveiling,* concerning Catholicism).

Due to the wavering nature of so many of today's

Protestant leaders as well as Catholicism and many other religions, the "forever" is taken out of hell and has been made into a temporary punishment. This modern idea is referred to as universalism.

Universalism

Universalism means that all men will ultimately arrive safely in heaven. According to the theory, because Christ died for all men, it stands to reason that all men will eventually be saved. Moreover, since all men were made sinners because of Adam, all men will be made alive because of Christ (I Cor. 15:22). This is a classic case of taking part and not all of Scripture for doctrine. For instance, in Revelation 20:10 we find that the Antichrist, a man, and the false prophet, also a man, are to be "...tormented day and night for ever and ever." This is the end of their story. Scripture does not teach that these men will ever be made alive in Christ. Forever means forever!

We do not have the luxury of selecting certain Scriptures to support what we conceive as truth. We must keep in mind that the usage of the word "all" is used many times in a restricted sense (see Matt. 3:5–6; Lk. 2:1; Jn. 3:26). Therefore, the word "all" sometimes has boundaries when kept in proper context. As far as universalism is concerned, consider Mark 3:29, in which Christ speaks of the unpardonable sin, or the "eternal sin." Matthew 12:32 records that "...whosoever speaketh against the Holy Ghost, it shall not be

112

forgiven him, neither in this world, neither in the world to come." That puts universalism in its proper category as false doctrine.

Annihilation: Man Burned Up

Another prevalent theory is that hell is real, but that it is complete annihilation. In a nutshell, it, too, takes the "forever" out of hell. The idea is that those cast into the literal burning fire are completely consumed and passed on into oblivion.

We have seen earlier that the word, *apollumi* (destroy) does not mean to annihilate (Matt. 10:28). Annihilation would be good news to the sinner if it were true. However, Christ taught that both the righteous and the unrighteous have eternal destinations:

"And these shall go away into everlasting punishment: but the righteous into life eternal" (Matt. 25:46).

The same Greek word is used in this verse for "everlasting" as for "eternal." That word is *aionios,* which means "forever." It only stands to reason that if heaven is "forever," then hell is "forever," too.

"And many of them that sleep in the dust of the earth shall awake, some to **everlasting** life, and some to shame and **everlasting** contempt" (Daniel 12:2).

The Hebrew word for everlasting is *owlam,* which means, "the vanishing point is concealed," or "eternal." Again, annihilation is not in the picture. We have seen that the Antichrist and the false prophet will be tormented day and night forever (Rev. 20:10). The same is true for those who receive the mark of the beast (Rev. 14:9–11). They will be tormented with fire and brimstone forever.

> "And the smoke of their torment ascendeth up **for ever and ever**: and they have no rest day nor night, who worship the beast and his image, and whosoever receiveth the mark of his name" (Revelation 14:11).

Hell is a place of continual torment. It is where "...their worm dieth not" (Mrk. 9:44,46,48). This does not refer to an earthworm, maggot or any such creature. It is "their" worm. This is a metaphoric semblance of a worm. It will be like the movement of a grub, earthworm or maggot in hot ashes: twisting and squirming with pain. In addition, there will be weeping (wailing) and gnashing (grinding) of teeth (Matt. 8:12; 22:13; 24:51; 25:30; Lk. 13:28) — also signs of extreme pain and suffering.

Hell is a place where the fire is never quenched (Mrk. 9:43,45,46,48). The word "fire" is found 83 times in 79 verses of the New Testament. It is translated from six Greek words that differ slightly in meaning:

phos – meaning "shine" or "lumination" (Mrk. 14:54; Lk. 22:54).

anthrakia – meaning "fire of coals" (Jn. 18:18, 21:9)

pura – meaning "a fire" (Acts 28:3, coming from *pur*).

phlogizol – meaning "to ignite" (James 3:6, second and third mention).

purinos – meaning "flaming" (Rev. 9:17).

pur – meaning "fire," that is, as ignited materials such as wood or gas or vapor that flames and causes heat.

The majority of words translated as "fire" in the New Testament is *pur*, a literal burning flame of fire. It must be noted that the intensity of the fire may range in degree. For instance, under natural conditions, the red flame is not as hot as the blue flame. The hottest known flame is completely black. This would align with the terms given concerning hell. Jesus referred to hell as "outer darkness" (Matt. 8:12; 22:13; 25:30). He also connects hell, and individuals who go there, with a flame of fire (Lk. 16:24), indicating a personal flame of fire for unsaved individuals. The word for fire in Mark 9:43–48 is *pur*, a literal, everlasting, burning flame of fire.

Does the Punishment Fit the Crime?

If the punishment does not seem to fit the crime, we must consider the severity of the crime. What if the greatness of sin is based upon the greatness of the one against whom it is committed? We cannot fully comprehend God's greatness; therefore, doubtless we can comprehend the gravity of sin against God. We do know that God does not take pleasure in the death of the wicked:

"For I have no pleasure in the death of him that dieth, saith the Lord GOD: wherefore turn yourselves, and live ye" (Ezekiel 18:32).

God does not want anyone to perish, but wants all men to come to repentance (II Peter 3:9). However, a holy God cannot tolerate wickedness (Psa. 11:5).

"For thou art not a God that hath pleasure in wickedness: neither shall evil dwell with thee" (Psalm 5:4).

We tend to forget that God is God and we are not. His ways are higher than ours (Isa. 55:8–9); therefore, we must completely trust His judgment for His judgment is true:

"A false balance is abomination to the LORD: but a just weight is his delight" (Proverbs 11:1).

Whatever the degree of punishment, it will fit the crime, because God is just. Imagine the wickedness of the world and how God has allowed untold misery for thousands of years. Why, then, would it be any different for Him to allow misery to continue forever?

"O the depth of the riches both of the wisdom and knowledge of God! how unsearchable are his judgments, and his ways past finding out!" (Romans 11:33).

Natives of the Bush

Many have stumbled over the notion that God would send to hell people who live in remote areas of the world who have never heard the Gospel of Christ. First of all, God would not and does not do that

116

(Rom. 2:7–16). In addition, we, as "civilized" people, cannot take the liberty of using those who are considered natives of the bush (or like peoples) as an excuse for a presumed flaw in God's plan. The Apostle Paul received a revelation concerning such people. The Holy Spirit instructed him to write of Jews, Christians, non-Christians, and particularly the so-called "natives of the bush." Concerning God's principle (or law) pertaining to His respect to all persons, Paul wrote:

"To them who by patient continuance in well doing seek for glory and honour and immortality, eternal life: But unto them that are contentious, and do not obey the truth, but obey unrighteousness, indignation and wrath, tribulation and anguish, upon every soul of man that doeth evil, of the Jew first, and also of the Gentile; But glory, honour, and peace, to every man that worketh good, to the Jew first, and also to the Gentile: **For there is no respect of persons with God.** For as many as have sinned without law shall also perish without law: and as many as have sinned in the law shall be judged by the law; (For not the hearers of the law are just before God, but the doers of the law shall be justified. **For when the Gentiles, which have not the law, do by nature the things contained in the law, these, having not the law, are a law unto themselves:** Which shew the work of the law written in their hearts, their conscience also bearing witness, and their thoughts the mean while accusing or else excusing one another;) In the day when God shall judge the secrets of men by Jesus Christ according to my gospel" (Romans 2:7–16).

In other words, certain people of Paul's day who lived in remote regions had not heard the Gospel of Christ. These people — in doing those things that are right and just because their conscience tells them what is right and just — are a law unto themselves. They will appear at the Judgment Seat of Christ for their reward. Some people fit that criteria today.

Is that an excuse for us? Should we be silent in our personal witness? Should we refrain from sending missionaries to these natives of the bush? No. We know that those who wish to do right will readily accept the salvation message. We should also know that many "unjust" people will respond to the message of Christ when they are presented with the opportunity. We should not be silent or refrain from our duty to spread God's Word.

Furthermore, people living in a "civilized" nation such as the United States have no excuse for not accepting the Gospel. We are a so-called "Christian" nation; the Gospel is presented by the week, by the day, by the hour and sometimes even by the minute. Church buildings exist in virtually every city, township and village in the United States. The witness of Christ reaches even into the most remote communities. Billboards, television, newspaper and computer media also serve as witnesses of Christ. Moreover, Christians are instructed to personally reach out to the lost throughout the world. It is up to each one of us to heed the call when such witnesses present themselves.

Hell Is Not Merely the Grave

Sheowl (hell) is translated as "the grave" approximately 31 times in Scripture. As with the English language, most all Hebrew and Greek words can mean different things, especially considering the context in which they are written. The word *sheowl* refers to paradise 34 additional times. In keeping with Scripture, the grave is the resting place for the body, not for the soul. We read about this under the heading, "Soul Sleep" in Chapter Five. Incidentally, the Jehovah's Witnesses are the most ardent supporters of "Soul Sleep," and have very extreme views concerning hell.

Hell for Jehovah's Witnesses

Jehovah's Witnesses believe that Christians are working under Satan's influence and therefore are spreading false doctrine. They consider it heresy to teach the existence of a literal burning hell. Their interpretation regarding this issue is appealing to many because it attempts to remove the eternal duration, the fire, and the torment from hell.

Jehovah's Witnesses contend that the soul is just another way of referring to one's whole being. Therefore, the soul ceases to exist after death, or, as we have read under "Soul Sleep." Death becomes nothing more than the extinction of being and necessitates a re-creation of the soul.

To the Jehovah's Witnesses, hell is nothing more than the burning garbage heap outside of Jerusalem.

Such a belief is obviously orchestrated by those who sincerely fear hell and deny scriptural truth. If I were in denial of the deity of Jesus (as evidenced by their removal of Christ's deity in the New World Translation) and believed in a works-oriented salvation, I would fear hell, too. These individuals need our prayers and the correct witness of Jesus Christ as Lord and Savior!

Jerusalem's Garbage Heap

Gehenna is the Greek word for "hell" and "punishment." It originates from two Hebrew words meaning, "valley of Hinnom." The valley of Hinnom, located south of Jerusalem, was used as the garbage dump for Jerusalem during Jesus' time. All of the filth and garbage of the city, including the dead bodies of animals and executed criminals, were thrown into this trash heap. Fires burned continuously in this area to consume the waste. Maggots and other creatures worked non-stop to help disintegrate the filth. Wild dogs howled and gnashed their teeth as they fought over the garbage. We can imagine how awful the stench must have been when winds blew over the city from the direction of this garbage heap.

This dump — located in a deep, narrow glen south of Jerusalem — was in the same valley where the Canaanites worshiped Baal and Molech, the fire-god, by sacrificing their children in a continuously burning fire. Even Ahaz and Manasseh, kings of Judah, were guilty of this idolatry (II Chron. 28:3; 33:6). It became a place of reproach and was therefore the perfect representation of a place of everlasting punishment, especially because of its fires.

The valley of Hinnom presents a perfect earthly depiction of the literal burning hell. That is to say, it serves as a type or symbol of the real thing. It would be preposterous to think that Jesus and the disciples would use Jerusalem's city dump as a scare tactic for the eternal souls of men.

Many times Jesus used objects, places and events to describe literal things. It becomes quite obvious when picturing the valley of Hinnom that Jesus mentioned this place only as a likeness of a literal hell. In addition, Jesus mentioned *"Gehenna"* in the context of eternal damnation (Matt. 23:33; Mrk. 9:44–48) and an eternal burning fire (Mrk. 9:43). The fire of Hinnom outside of Jerusalem is not and has never been a place of eternal damnation, nor has its fires been eternal.

Predestined for Hell

Many people believe in the doctrine of predestination. This is the belief that certain individuals are predestined to go to heaven and others are predestined to go to hell, regardless of one's actions toward God. Some events are definitely predestined in Scripture, such as: the Garden, the Flood, the Church Age, the Second Coming of Christ, and so on.

However, Scripture does not reveal that certain people have been predestined to go to heaven or hell. Man has always had a free will to accept or reject God's plan of salvation.

We have had a choice in every dispensation since Adam. How would one actually know whether he was chosen for heaven or for hell, especially if his actions toward God were not a factor? How would one know if he was chosen or not if it's by faith that we accept what God has said? Those who believe this doctrine explain that those who have been predestined to hell naturally reject the true path, and those who have been predestined for heaven naturally accept Christ. That sounds good, but it is an unreasonable and untrue depiction of Scripture. Why? Because every man is given light.

He Lighteth Every Man

Jesus said, "No man can come to me, except the Father which hath sent me draw him"(Jn. 6:44). Jesus was explaining His Deity in this verse. This we know because every man has some degree of calling and light:

"That was the true Light, which lighteth **every man that come into the world**" (John 1:9).

So every man in the world has been given some degree of light by God; therefore, he has the opportunity to be saved. In John 12:32,33, Jesus said,

"And I, if I be lifted up from the earth, **will draw all men** unto me. This he said, signifying what death he should die" (John 12:32–33).

When Jesus draws "all" men to Him, then any one of "all" men could be saved. Even nature causes men to seek God (Psa. 19:1–4). This means that all men have a choice to accept or reject God's plan of salvation.

"God...now commandeth **all men** every where to repent" (Acts 17:30).

God does not command people to do what He has made impossible for them to do.

God's Elect

It is true that the saved are God's elect, "chosen...in him before the foundation of the world" (Eph. 1:4). But it is wrong to make this election a whim whereby God saves some and damns others. We have already seen that the word "all" must be kept in its proper context. Many times it is limited in its usage; however, if any particular passage specifically uses and distinguishes that every man is given light, and that the word "all" refers to every man concerning the salvation offered, we can rest assured that every individual has the opportunity to be saved. We need not fear that we are of those who are predestined to be lost and forever separated from God. Consider Paul's message to Timothy concerning salvation:

"...who is the Saviour of **all men**, specially of those that believe" (I Timothy 4:10).

This means that He is "specially" a personal Savior for those who believe and even a potential Savior for those who might believe:

"For this is good and acceptable in the sight of God our Saviour; Who will have **all men** to be saved, and to come unto the knowledge of the truth" (I Timothy 2:3,4).

It is God's will that all be saved. But because of man's sinful nature, we know that this has not happened and will not happen because many people choose not to follow God. In addition, we have seen previously that, "...there is no respect of persons with God" (Rom. 2:11). Even the heathen who have not heard the Gospel are called to God by nature and by the law of their own hearts, as discussed earlier. The souls of men are only predestined in the sense that some will definitely end up in hell and others in heaven. However, these destinations are reached only by each individual's God-given choice, not by God's predetermined blessing or curse.

The Dead

Those who are yet in their sins are referred to as being among the "dead" (Eph. 2:1–5); they are spiritually dead (I Cor. 2:14). To die physically while remaining in that condition seals the plight of hell.

Hades is a place of torment for the holding of

those who are called the "dead" (Rev. 20:12); it is not the place for the "dead IN Christ." The "dead" will be resurrected from Hades, brought before the Great White Throne and judged according to their works. This judgment will reveal that their names were never recorded in the Lamb's Book of Life. Those so judged will be cast into the Lake of Fire. This is the everlasting stage of hell, the second death. How about this for a sobering thought? The second death has no resurrection. None!

You may have heard the saying, "Born once, die twice — born twice, die once." In other words, if you have only experienced a physical birth then you will die twice: the physical death, which will be followed by the second death. However, if you have experienced physical birth and have been born again of the Spirit of God you will only die once (the only exception being those taken in the Rapture of the Church).

> "And death and hell were cast into the lake of fire. This is the second death. And whosoever was not found written in the book of life was cast into the lake of fire" (Revelation 20:14–15).

The Reality of Hell

Although many argue that hell is not a literal place with literal torment, the rich man of Luke 16:19–31 would strongly disagree. A brief study of this passage reveals the reality and severity of hell. This narrative was directed toward the religionists of the day.

The sneers from the Pharisees gave birth to this most solemn narrative from Jesus concerning the rich man and Lazarus. These religious leaders were self-centered and living within the bondage of the love of money and all it could buy. Their sinful and selfish desires stood between them and God. The example of the rich man and Lazarus was given to teach these religionists, and indeed all of us, the fate of those who trust in self indulgence and live according to the lust of the flesh. Moreover, the narrative teaches us the destiny of those who trust in Christ.

The rich man, called Dives (Latin for "rich man"), had fared sumptuously every day. Lazarus was a beggar who desired the crumbs from his table. When Lazarus died, he was immediately carried into Abraham's bosom; when the rich man died, he immediately went to hell. The rich man did not go to hell because he was rich, nor did Lazarus go to paradise because he was poor. Our relationship with God, not our status in life, determines our eternal destination. The rich man had rejected the opportunity to have a relationship with God.

It wasn't Jesus' custom to use names in His parables. Here, however, He used the name of Lazarus and made reference to Abraham, Moses and Hades. Therefore, the story of the rich man and Lazarus is based on more than just a parable; it is based upon actual events and actual people.

In Chapter One we discussed the subject of body, soul, and spirit. Although Dives' body was no doubt in the grave or in a hewn tomb somewhere, his soul retained all of the feelings and emotions of his physical body. He felt his torment in a flame (*phlox* — a blaze). He could see across the great gulf between Hades and paradise (which at this time was still in the lower parts of the Earth).

The rich man could experience thirst (v.24) and could remember events on Earth (v.25). He also felt compassion for his family (v. 28). Although he was without God, he was made in the image of God; thus, he possessed an eternal soul with eternal properties.

The longevity of this rich man's plight is suggested in Abraham's reply concerning his brothers. The rich man had requested that Lazarus return to testify to his five brothers, "...lest they also come into this place of torment." The reply was, "...they have Moses and the prophets; let them hear them."

This suggests that Dives had arrived at the torments of *sheowl* (Hades) many years before Jesus told them about the event. Abraham said, "...let them *hear* them." The word "hear" is *akouo*, which means, "to be noised." Therefore, his brothers could "hear" the voices of Moses and the prophets. If that is the case, then Dives had been in *sheowl* approximately 1,400 years when Jesus told the Pharisees about his fate. It's been more than 2,000 years since Christ told of the rich man's fate. Thus, this man has been in *sheowl* (Hades) for roughly 3,400 years. This is only one testimony to the duration of hell.

When Lazarus died, he was carried by angels to Abraham's bosom. Dives could see Lazarus in Abraham's bosom. As we saw earlier, "Abraham's bosom" was the reference of Old Testament saints for the destination of the faithful dead. This was a tender expression of laying one's head on the bosom of a loving father. (It is very likely that Abraham is being used here as a type of God speaking to the rich man).

It is reasonable to think that Lazarus' body was entombed or buried somewhere and returning to dust in the Earth from where it came. His spirit had returned to God upon the death of his physical body. His soul was at rest in the paradise side of Hades until Jesus' resurrection. As seen earlier, when Jesus arose from the dead He led "captivity captive," thus, Lazarus is now enjoying the peaceful rest in the Sea of Glass, contently awaiting the resurrection. God's plan for mankind is awesome!

Dear friend, hell is real; it is prepared for the devil and his angels. It is an eternal lake of literal, burning fire. Whether we like to admit it or not, the punishment fits the crime for those who go there. God doesn't send anyone to hell, so please do not choose to go there by rejecting the way of escape that has been provided through Christ.

We have revealed the plan of salvation in this chapter. If you haven't accepted the Lord Jesus Christ into your life, please do so now (II Cor. 6:2). Several mentions have been made throughout this book about how to be saved from the curse of sin, death, and hell. It is of utmost importance that we heed God's call for salvation. Eternity is forever and ever without end! Ω

The Path to Eternity

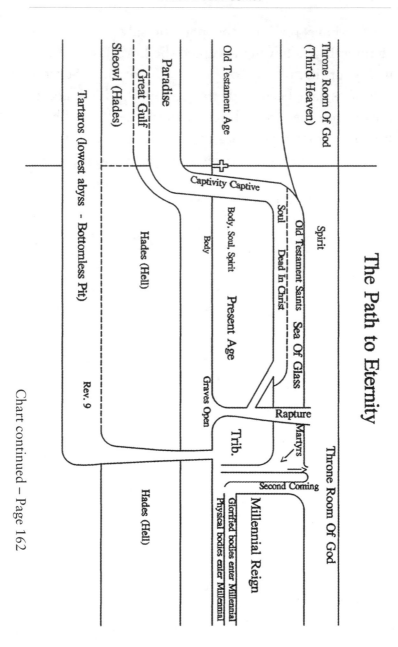

Throne Room Of God (Third Heaven)

Old Testament Age

Paradise

Great Gulf

Sheowl (Hades)

Tartaros (lowest abyss - Bottomless Pit)

Captivity Captive

Spirit

Old Testament Saints

Soul

Dead In Christ

Sea Of Glass

Body, Soul, Spirit

Body

Present Age

Hades (Hell)

Graves Open

Rev. 9

Rapture

Trib.

Martyrs

Second Coming

Hades (Hell)

Throne Room Of God

Millennial Reign

Glorified bodies enter Millennial

Physical bodies enter Millennial

Chart continued – Page 162

130

CHAPTER
7

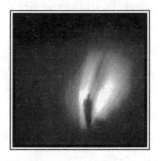

SUICIDE

No matter how noble it may seem, how prudent it may appear, or how sacrificial it is, there
is no honor in taking one's own life.

One suicide occurs approximately every forty seconds. Suicide leaves nothing but weariness of spirit and oppression of the soul for those who have been left behind. Nothing can leave such a scar on the heart than to have a loved one conclude that life is not worth living, that life's heaviest burden was to have nothing left to carry.

I wish no harm or hurt to befall anyone because of what may be said in this chapter. I approach this subject with the greatest respect and the deepest sympathy for those families who bear the burden left to them by loved ones who have committed suicide. I do write, however, without favor toward friend or foe, but simply for the truth concerning this terrible method of death.

Out of What?

Suicide has now reached epidemic proportions. National statistics estimate that 11 out of every 100,000 people take their own lives. This is alarming, but it comes as no surprise. Books that explain how to commit suicide are selling at an enormous rate and it stands to reason that many who purchase them follow through by ending their lives.

Apparently these people are looking for an easy way out, but out of what? If suicide were an acceptable method of death before Creator God, and if it were a faster avenue to heaven, Christians would be taking advantage of this self-glory route by the millions. Job said that man's days are few and full of trouble, so why go through all the trouble and heartache if you have an opportunity to get to heaven quicker? Well, that's not the case.

God did not ordain suicide. It actually hastens the consequences of eternal existence. We saw earlier that annihilation is not in the picture for humans because we are eternal creatures. That makes suicide serious business, eternally serious business.

Suicide robs God of the purpose for which the life was given. Paul said:

> "I am crucified with Christ: **nevertheless I live**; yet not I, but Christ liveth in me: **and the life which I now live in the flesh I live by the faith of the Son of God,** who loved me, and gave himself for me" (Galatians 2:20).

Whose life is it anyway? Don't we have a right to take our own life if that is what we choose to do? The fact is that we do not have that right under any circumstances. We are not our own; we belong to God. We were bought with a price at Calvary by the blood of Jesus.

> "For ye are bought with a price: therefore glorify God in your body, and in your spirit, which are God's" (I Corinthians 6:20).

Although some people believe that suicide enables them to control their own destiny, that goal is an impossible task. It's true that we may end our lives, but death is not a destiny, it's only the beginning. We saw earlier that the spirit and soul continue to live after the body dies. Moreover, at some point (whether saved or lost), the body will be resurrected to once again accompany the soul.

We also discussed the fact that only two destinations are prescribed for eternal existence. These destinations are unchangeable. They were created that way and will remain so according to God's plan.

Choosing our own way is not good. "There is a way which seemeth right unto a man, but the end thereof are the ways of death" (Pro. 14:12; 16:25). There is no provision in Scripture for us to make our own way to heaven. To do so would void the sacrifice made on the cross of Calvary. In addition, it would void the very purpose for which we were created.

God, as Creator, has the power over all existence. Therefore, if we feel our usefulness has expired and we wish to die, we must appeal to God for death. To welcome death from the hand of God is an acceptable plea, but it is not acceptable to force the hand that brings it. If He chooses to leave us here, then we must serve in whatever capacity our ability allows. It is God alone who should control life, whether it continues or stops. Job said:

> "...Naked came I out of my mother's womb, and naked shall I return thither: the LORD gave, and the LORD hath taken away; blessed be the name of the LORD. In all this Job sinned not, nor charged God foolishly" (Job 1:21–22).

The last action of those who commit suicide is murder. Does that mean that this act against God is unpardonable? The only way I know how to handle this matter is through the examples given in Scripture. Let's see what we can learn from the passages in Scripture that mention suicide.

We find five accounts of suicide: King Saul; Saul's servant; Zimri; Ahithophel; and Judas. Abimelech is the one assisted suicide case that we find in the Bible. We must note that Samson's death was an act of war against the enemy by which he died; it is not to be considered a suicide.

King Saul

The people of Israel desired to have a king lead them to victory over the Philistines (I Sam. 9:16). They simply did not trust God for the victory (I Sam. 10:18–19). During this troublesome time, a young man and his servant had gone to look for his father's wandering livestock. This young man's name was Saul. After much searching, Saul finally came to where Samuel, God's prophet and Israel's religious leader, lived. God had told Samuel that such a man would come and would be the one chosen by God to become Israel's first king.

Samuel heard from the Lord again upon seeing Saul. Saul was the man of whom God had spoken (I Sam. 9:17); therefore, Saul, the son of Kish, became the first king over Israel (I Sam. 9:2; 31:12; I Chron.

5:10; 26:28).

Saul was a large and attractive man (I Sam. 9:2; 10:23) who stood head and shoulders above everyone else. He also was anointed and filled with the Spirit of God (I Sam. 10:1,9; 11:6). In his early years, Saul was humble and practiced self-control (I Sam. 10:22; 10:27; 11:13); it wasn't until later that he became conceited and self-reliant.

Saul was from the tribe of Benjamin, which was located on the borders of the northern and southern kingdoms of Israel. This placement gave him acceptance from both kingdoms of Israel. Soon after his anointing, Saul became bold in leadership and was deemed a great military leader. Saul had many victories on behalf of his people in his early years.

Saul had several admirable qualities, but patience wasn't one of them. Impatience prompted him to act foolishly apart from the will of God. This cost him dearly. One crucial mistake that he made was not heeding the instructions of God's prophet. Samuel had told Saul that he must wait for him in Gilgal for seven days, at which time Samuel would come and offer sacrifices and give instruction from God (I Sam. 10:8).

Samuel arrived late on the seventh day, but Saul acted impatiently by offering the sacrifices in direct disobedience to God. In addition, Saul had determined in his heart to engage the Philistines without the God-given instructions from Samuel.

Saul must have known that waiting for Samuel was important or else he wouldn't have made so many excuses when Samuel arrived (I Sam. 10:11). He also "ran to salute him," revealing a boastful attempt to impress Samuel for what he had done.

It's one thing to disobey God's instruction, and another to boast about it. When Saul realized that something was amiss, he tried to blame Samuel (v.11). Samuel readily replied,

"...Thou hast done foolishly: thou hast not kept the commandment of the LORD thy God, which he commanded thee: for now would the LORD have established thy kingdom upon Israel for ever" (I Samuel 13:13).

Saul's actions were in direct conflict with God's will. Moreover, Saul was unrepentant. (Sinning is not what brings man to ruin; sinning and not repenting is what brings man to ruin.)

On another occasion, the Lord instructed Saul through Samuel to wage war against the Amalekites. Saul was commanded to kill all men, women, infants and nursing children. This command included killing all of the oxen, sheep, camels and donkeys (I Sam. 15:3). But Saul spared King Agag and saved the best animals. Upon his return, Saul lied to Samuel by telling him that he had followed his instructions to the letter (I Sam. 15:10–11).

Note: The Amalekites were bitter foes of Israel. Because of their treacherous attacks, Moses declared that God would continually wage war against them (Ex. 17:14–16). The command was to be a judgment against the Amalekites and a purification of the land. As a result of Saul's disobedience, the Amalekites continued to plague Israel.

The Lord told Samuel that Saul had turned back from following Him. These actions cost Saul his kingdom (I Sam. 15:23). His rebellion was equivalent to the sin of witchcraft, and his stubbornness was as iniquity and idolatry. Saul repented, but his words were empty. In his prayer he said that he feared the people and obeyed their voices. This was totally out of character for this great leader. Samuel evidently recognized this bogus act of repentance:

> "And Saul said unto Samuel, I have sinned: for I have transgressed the commandment of the LORD, and thy words: because I feared the people, and obeyed their voice. Now therefore, I pray thee, pardon my sin, and turn again with me, that I may worship the LORD. And Samuel said unto Saul, I will not return with thee: for thou hast rejected the word of the LORD, and the LORD hath rejected thee from being king over Israel" (I Samuel 15:24–26).

Although he had brought the consequences upon himself, Saul would not accept the word of the Lord. He did not want to be replaced by another king. As Samuel turned to leave, Saul tore his mantle and cried out again in repentance. This time his repentance was true and Samuel acknowledged it (I Sam. 15:31). However, the results of the sin remained and Saul's kingdom was given to someone who would be a better king (I Sam. 15:28). This "better" king was David.

Saul revealed yet another undesirable trait when Samuel anointed David. Jealousy boiled up in him to the point that he sought to kill David (I Sam. 18:8; 19:1). Sincere repentance brings forgiveness, but the effects of our sin may linger to haunt us. We must be cautious not to have a lack of commitment when we repent. True repentance brings true commitment. Such a lack often leads to greater sins, as it did with Saul.

On yet another occasion, Saul called out to the Lord, but the Lord didn't answer as quickly as Saul thought He should. Therefore, Saul went to the witch of Endor for answers (I Sam. 28:6–7). His impatience and self-will were the seeds that led to his downfall and eventual ruin (I Sam. 13:12–13). Saul's sin caused the Spirit of the Lord to depart from him (I Sam. 16:14).

Consulting "familiar spirits" opens one up to the possibility of becoming possessed by demonic spirits. Many times this causes bouts of madness. We saw an example of this in the account of the man at the tombs of Gadarene (Mrk. 5:1–5). It is also evident in Saul's continued disobedience and rash vows (I Sam. 15:11–23).

The Philistines had heard of both Israel's failing king and prosperity. Once again, the Philistines attacked the Hebrew nation. At this time, Saul's three sons were killed. Wounded in battle, Saul committed suicide by falling upon his sword when his servant refused to take his life (I Sam. 31:4).

It is evident that Saul had a rebellious nature. He lacked the ability to share power and popularity. He was a king who had great opportunity, but was full of pride and egotism so he abused the power entrusted to him. In addition, he lacked true commitment in his repentance. This led to moral degradation, ruin and eventual suicide. This act even became a catalyst for yet another suicide.

Saul's Servant

After Saul killed himself, his servant did the same thing (I Sam. 31:4–5). One possible reason for this could be fear of the enemy. Or it could have been due to his sense of failure in carrying out the king's request. No doubt Saul's servant had been influenced by Saul during his reign. He obviously shared many of the same convictions and sentiments, even to death. We never know just what kind of influence we have until it's too late.

Zimri

Before Zimri became Israel's fifth king (I Kings 16:8–20), he was a servant of King Elah and a commander of half of his chariots. Zimri had conspired against Elah, and upon occasion, while Elah was carousing in drunkenness, Zimri killed Elah and proclaimed himself to be king. Therefore, he secured his place of authority by murder. His first act as king was to slay all those who were in the house of Baasha.

King Elah's army, under Omri, was in battle at Gibbethon at the time of Elah's death. However, when the army heard that the king was dead, they proclaimed their general, Omri, as king. Now Israel had two kings: one self-proclaimed and one who was appointed. When Omri heard about Elah's assassination, he abandoned the siege at Gibbethon and besieged the capital city of Tirzah. There Zimri had retreated to the innermost part of Elah's palace. When Zimri saw that the city had been besieged by Omri, he "...burned the king's house down upon himself" (I Kings 16:18). Thus, Zimri's self-appointed reign lasted only seven days (I Kings 16:15).

Ahithophel

Ahithophel, one of King David's counselors, was so highly regarded that his advice was given the respect and authority of a divine oracle (II Sam. 16:23). However, Ahithophel assisted Absalom, David's son, in his revolt against King David. It is evident that Ahithophel was trying to rise to power through Absalom, because he knew that Absalom was favored by the people (II Sam. 15:12). When Absalom rebelled against David, Ahithophel apparently believed his own popularity would bring success to Absalom's revolt. In an attempt to usher in

Absalom's reign, Ahithophel advised Absalom to take David's harem (II Sam. 15:12; 16:21). This act was equivalent to claiming the throne. He also advised Absalom to pursue David, who had fled Jerusalem. But Absalom chose to listen to Hushai, who had advised the prince not to pursue his father. Sensing that Absalom's rebellion was doomed, Ahithophel hanged himself (II Sam. 17:23).

Abimelech and Assisted Suicide

Abimelech was the king of Shechem, the first capital city of Israel's northern kingdom (Jdg. 9:6). After Gideon's death, the children of Israel had quickly returned to worshipping idols. During this time, Abimelech conspired with his mother's family to secure his kingship.

Abimelech's campaign included speaking against the 70 sons of Jerubbaal. His argument was whether the Shechemites wanted 70 to rule over them or only one, namely, himself. Not only did he conspire with his influential in-laws, he used the persuasion of being a "brother" to the Shechemites (Jdg. 9:2–3). The plan worked and soon Abimilech was made king (Jdg. 9:6).

The people of Shechem gave Abimelech 70 pieces of silver from the house of Baalberith, a Shechemite god. He took the silver and hired some "...vain and light persons" to help him carry out his evil intent. He and his men killed 69 of the 70 sons of Jerubbaal. Only Jotham escaped (Jdg. 9:5).

The kingship of Abimelech was rebuked by Jotham, who referred to Abimelech as a "bramble bush." Jotham also predicted that an awful fate would befall Abimelech (Jdg. 9:20).

After he reigned for three years, internal strife began to flow. "God sent an evil spirit between Abimelech and the men of Shechem," and "...they dealt treacherously with Abimelech." There were several attempts to overtake the throne, but all of them failed (Jdg. 9:30–40). In one instance, Abimelech and his army gathered tree branches and burned 1,000 men and women of Shechem in the temple of Baal-berith, thought to be a sanctuary from the wrath of Abimelech (Jdg. 9:48–49).

Finally the day came for the fulfillment of Jotham's curse. After burning the 1,000 men and women in the temple of Baal-berith, Abimelech besieged the town of Thebez and took possession of it. The inhabitants took refuge in a strong tower within the city. As Abimelech approached the door of the tower to set it on fire, a woman threw a piece of millstone upon him and crushed his skull. Abimelech knew that he was dying, so he called for his armor-bearer and said, "Draw thy sword, and slay me, that men say not of me, A woman slew him. And his young man thrust him through, and he died" (Jdg. 9:54, 56,57).

Judas Iscariot

The most famous suicide in Scripture is that of

Judas Iscariot. Judas was one of the twelve chosen to be with Christ during His earthly ministry (Mrk. 3:14). His name is always mentioned last in the lists of the disciples, probably because of the stigma with which his death and his betrayal of Christ have been associated.

Each mention of Judas in Scripture carries the distinction of dishonor in a most pointed way: "...sought opportunity to betray him," "...who also betrayed him [Jesus]," "...which also was a traitor," and so on (Matt. 10:4; 26:16; Mrk. 3:19; Lk. 6:16; Jn. 18:2,5).

Jesus came to fulfill the Old Testament Law, begin a new era, and draw a distinction between Law and Grace. The Age of Grace is also called the Church Age, as discussed in Chapter Three of this book. Jesus and the twelve disciples lived during the time of transition between the Age of the Law and the Church Age. On the Day of Pentecost, shortly after this time of transition, the Spirit of God began to live within the hearts of all those who accepted Jesus Christ as Lord. We saw earlier that before the Day of Pentecost, the Spirit of God worked within individuals who were specifically chosen for the Lord's work. Such was the case with the apostles, including Judas Iscariot.

The stigma associated with Judas has caused many to contend that he was of the devil from the very onset and was doomed without a chance of repentance; however, this is not the case. Judas was chosen by

Christ and ordained to be a disciple. He was evidently found among the followers of Christ, from whom he was chosen. Like the other eleven who were chosen by Christ, Judas was empowered by the Holy Spirit (Matt. 10:20). He was also an ambassador of the Gospel, called an apostle (Matt. 10:1–2). In addition, he was recognized with the twelve as one of the sheepfold (Matt. 10:16). Judas, along with the rest of the eleven, was empowered to cast out devils and was given authority over sickness and disease (Matt. 10:1–8; Mrk. 3:14–19; 6:7; Lk. 9:1–2). He was also commissioned and ordained to preach (Matt. 10:27; 11:1; Mrk. 3:14).

Although Scripture does not say that Judas called Jesus "Lord," he did address him as "Rabbi" (Matt. 26:25). However, such lack of recognition is not enough evidence to prove that Judas was not as "saved" as the rest of the twelve, for he was of the sheepfold (Matt. 10:16). The same can be said of Nicodemus, for he only referred to Jesus as "Rabbi." Yet Nicodemus defended Jesus before the Pharisees (Jn. 7:50) and was one of the men who brought precious spices for Jesus' burial (Jn. 19:39).

We must not take lightly the choosing of Judas by Jesus as one of the twelve. Jesus must have seen potential in Judas or else He would not have chosen him and commissioned him for the work of the Kingdom. Additionally, Jesus would not have ordained a demon-possessed man to do righteousness — an imperfect man, yes, but not one who was possessed by a demon. For Judas to be a devil from the onset would contradict Jesus' teaching (Matt. 12:26; Mrk. 3:23). (This does not say, however, that a person who has been chosen for the Lord's work cannot become possessed by the devil, as we will soon learn).

Yes, Judas betrayed Christ, but it's easy to look back and point an accusing finger at Judas as the appointed "son of perdition." All twelve disciples were given warnings against denying the Lord Jesus (Matt. 10:33). All of them were warned against giving in and giving up and not enduring to the end (Matt. 10:22). Judas was aware of this. He wasn't singled out for these warnings.

The betrayal of Jesus was prophesied (Jn. 17:12; Psa. 109:7–8), but this preordained position does not imply that it must be Judas who would betray Christ. Peter also could have become such a man. Remember, Peter denied Christ three times, once even to the point of cursing. The office of betrayal was appointed, but twelve candidates were available to fill that position.

The difference between Judas and Peter is that Peter repented to the Lord and Judas did not. It's not so much in the flaws we possess, it's how we address them and what we do to correct them.

Problem Source

Jesus revealed the source of Judas' problems in

John 6:70: "Have not I chosen you twelve, and one of you is a devil?" The word "devil" here is *diabolos,* which means "a traducer (one who speaks maliciously), a false accuser and slanderer." In most instances, *diabolos* refers to Satan and his character; however, in this instance, it refers only to the characteristics of the devil. We know this is the case because Judas was not Satan himself, or else Satan would not have had to enter into him (Lk. 22:3). Thus, by definition, Judas was one who spoke spitefully, accusingly and slanderously against others. He was a follower of Christ, yet he had great flaws. Although he was commissioned for the Lord's work, Judas was judgmental and self-centered. Left unharnessed, these traits blossomed in a most unpleasant way. Judas' story drives home the truth that it is a must to practice self-control.

Apparently Judas nurtured rather than harnessed his imperfections. One such example is revealed in the scene at Bethany (Matt. 26:6–16; Mrk. 14:3–9), where we find the woman who anointed Jesus with precious ointment. Her warm outpouring of love was met with indignation from all of the disciples (Matt. 26:8). In a nutshell, her actions were not prudent and did not fit their perception of righteousness. Jesus rebuked them by relating that what she had done was not a bad thing but a good thing.

Although all twelve of the disciples were displeased with the woman's assumed wastefulness, it was Judas who expressed judgment and disrespect. His words portrayed little or no regard for the woman's feelings and intent. It's one thing to have an evil thought, but it's another to nurture that thought until it becomes an outward expression (James 1:19–20). He argued that the ointment could have been sold and the money given to the poor.

We know from Scripture that Judas had ulterior motives behind his speech at Bethany. This is realized by John's words in referring to Judas as a thief:

> "Then saith one of his disciples, Judas Iscariot, Simon's son, which should betray him, Why was not this ointment sold for three hundredpence, and given to the poor? **This he said, not that he cared for the poor; but because he was a thief, and had the bag, and bare what was put therein**" (John 12:4–6).

Judas went from judgmental self-centeredness to complete indignation. Masked behind the plea of care for the poor, he uncovered his personal vice, the love of money. Judas was the treasurer and keeper of monies for Jesus and the twelve. He apparently was given this task so that he might overcome this deep-rooted problem. Many times we are placed in positions that cause us to face our problems so that we will work them out.

Judas' indignation escalated to reproach. This reproach soon became bitter action. From the time of the Bethany scene, Judas set it in his heart to betray Jesus (Matt. 26:16). This action also reveals another of

Judas' character flaws: impatience.

There have been many suggestions as to why Judas betrayed Christ:

*Some say that he was jealous of the other disciples.

*Many contend that it was the inevitable outcome of Jesus' ministry that made him turn to the chief priests in order to save his own skin.

*Some have suggested that Judas might have been convinced that Jesus was a false Messiah, and that the true Messiah was yet to come.

*Others say that Judas may have been upset over what appeared to be an indifference to the law and Jesus' association with sinners.

Many such suggestions have been made in an attempt to understand Judas' betrayal of Jesus. We will see shortly that the evidence suggests a greater scheme.

Although it is difficult to understand why Judas betrayed Jesus, we can see that Judas allowed his judgmental character and self-centeredness to flourish into what John labeled "thievery." Greed is often a spring-board to disaster.

It is because of greed that a likely reason for Judas' betrayal of Jesus emerges. First, what is unlikely is that

Judas would betray Christ for only 30 pieces of silver, which was approximately one month's wages. Although this was gain, it wasn't enough of a gain to betray Jesus to the point of execution.

It is also unlikely that Judas deemed Christ a false Messiah and wished to stop Him.

All of the evidence reveals that Judas believed Christ was the Messiah. In fact, he even tried to force Jesus to take His earthly kingdom and overthrow Rome. He did this by betraying Him to the chief priests and elders. We know that the thought of an earthly kingdom was predominant in the minds of the apostles, even after the resurrection (Acts 1:6).

Thirty pieces of silver would have been just enough to convince the chief priests and elders that Judas was sincere in the betrayal. It would also accomplish the goal of a kingdom full of money when Jesus assumed the throne. As treasurer, Judas would stand to gain access to much more than 30 pieces of silver. A mind that plots against others will plot in favor of self, especially when such plotting is sure to bring great gain.

Judas' transgression was like that of a snowball rolling down a large embankment: the farther it went, the larger it became. The Greek word here for "transgression" is *parabaino,* meaning "to go contrary to; to violate a command."

"And they prayed, and said, Thou, Lord, which knowest the hearts of all men, show whether of these two (Joseph —

Matthias) thou hast chosen, That he may **take part of this ministry and apostleship, from which Judas by transgression fell,** that he might go to his own place" (Acts 1:24–25) (parenthesis mine).

Judas was walking in the flesh and looking at the world from the outside in.

We saw Judas at the Passover feast; his feet were washed and he heard Jesus say, "Ye are clean, but not all" (Jn. 13:10). Jesus also said, "...one of you shall betray me." Judas asked, "Is it I?"

Satan entered Judas after he had dipped the sop with Jesus (Jn. 13:27). Judas had been toying with the devil up to this point, but then the devil took full possession. After that, Judas was a disciple no more (Matt. 26:20; Jn. 13:26–30):

> "And he answered and said, He that dippeth his hand with me in the dish, the same shall betray me. The Son of man goeth as it is written of him: but woe unto that man by whom the Son of man is betrayed! it had been good for that man if he had not been born. Then Judas, which betrayed him, answered and said, Master, is it I? He said unto him, Thou hast said" (Matthew 26:23–25).

Shortly after the feast, Judas brought a band of officers and servants to the Garden where Jesus and the disciples were. In this Garden, Judas furthered his betrayal with a kiss (Matt. 26:47– 49; Mrk. 14:43–45; Lk. 22:47, 48; Jn. 18:1–5).

Judas' Reflection

It is evident that upon seeing Jesus condemned,

Judas had time for reflection. Instead of Jesus taking the kingdom, the kingdom (Rome) had taken Jesus. Judas was conscience-stricken when he realized this.

> "Then Judas, which had betrayed him, when he saw that he was condemned, repented himself, and brought again the thirty pieces of silver to the chief priests and elders, Saying, I have sinned in that I have betrayed the innocent blood. And they said, What is that to us? see thou to that. And he cast down the pieces of silver in the temple, and departed, and went and hanged himself" (Matthew 27:3–5).

The actions that followed prove further that Judas was trying to force Jesus into taking His earthly kingdom. He tried to reverse what had occurred. The money was not important; his standing with the chief priests and the elders was not important. Judas repented to himself and to the chief priests and elders, but not to Jesus. He could have cried out to God, but he did not. The devil's possession of him obstructed his one way of escape. Jesus had repeatedly told the twelve, "I am the Way." Judas knew this, but possession and self-centeredness blocked his path toward true repentance. He could not see beyond his guilt.

Judas' Suicide

By this time, Judas had allowed his heart to be corrupted to the point that all reason and rationale were gone. He had become possessed by the devil and saw no recourse but to take his own life. Had he only repented to the Lord or held on until after the resurrection, but he did not. He felt certain that he was indeed the "the son of perdition" (Jn. 17:12) without the choice of repentance, so he committed suicide. Judas "...departed and went and hanged himself" (Matt. 27:5). As a result, he chose his own destination; he went "...to his own place" (Acts 1:18–25 — discussed later).

Suicide Reflection

We have examined five instances of suicide and one instance of assisted suicide in Scripture. From these examples, we may draw some conclusions concerning the plight of those who commit suicide. We must keep in mind that four of the five suicides were committed under Old Testament Law and one during the time of transition between the ages of Law and Grace.

Let's look at these examples for comparison and lessons:

1. Saul

Positive Traits:
a. was chosen by God
b. was anointed and filled with the Spirit
c. was humble and practiced self control in early years
d. displayed bold leadership as king
Negative Traits:
a. was impatient

b. was self-willed and boastful

c. blamed others

d. was stubborn in repentance

e. consulted a witch

f. had the Spirit of God depart from him

g. was full of pride, jealousy, egotism

h. abused his power as king

i. fell upon his sword and committed suicide

2. Saul's Servant

Positive Traits:

a. was devoted to the king

Negative Traits:

a. held sense of failure due to disobeying the king

b. followed the example of the king by committing suicide

3. Zimri

Positive Traits:

a. none recorded

Negative Traits:

a. murdered king Elah

b. proclaimed himself as king

c. committed suicide by burning down the palace around himself

4. Ahithophel

Positive Traits:

a. was highly regarded as King David's advisor

Negative Traits:

a. plotted against King David with Absalom

b. revolted against the king for personal gain

c. hanged himself due to impending doom

5. Judas Iscariot

Positive Traits:

a. was found among the disciples of Christ

b. was chosen by Christ as an apostle

c. was anointed to preach

d. was anointed to heal and cast out demons

Negative Traits:

a. had a diabolical heart

b. became judgmental and self-centered

c. nurtured thoughts of spite, accusations and slander

d. was greedy

e. was a thief

f. plotted against Christ for self-gratification

g. became possessed by the devil

h. was non-repentant

i. hanged himself

When we study each of these people, we find only two who were directly called by God for His service (Saul –Judas), two who were closely associated with those called by God (Saul's servant – Ahithophel) and one who had no positive traits recorded (Zimri). We see one mention of assisted suicide (Abimelech).

The common thread in each of these cases is that

each individual had problems with self — whether it was a sense of pride, a sense of failure, or both. Problems with ourselves are major symptoms of those who look at the world from the outside in, as we read in Chapter Three.

When we compare ourselves with the people in the world around us, we often lean toward pride or pity. Many people are too proud to humble themselves to God's will and others are so down on themselves that they are convinced that God will not save them. The Bible tells us to deny ourselves and follow Jesus (Matt. 16:24), whatever our opinion of ourselves may be.

According to God's Word, those who have never repented to the Lord Jesus of their sins and who die in that condition already have sealed their fate. It matters not whether the death was because of sickness, homicide, suicide, an accident, a terrorist attack, natural causes, or self-sacrifice. But this does not necessarily apply to Saul and Judas. They were chosen by God, had accepted God's calling, and were anointed by God for service. Yet they committed suicide. Therefore, their cases add certain elements to our study that those of Saul's servant, Zimri and Ahithophel do not.

Son of Perdition

After Satan entered Judas and he had gone out to betray Jesus, in His prayer, Jesus labeled Judas the "son of perdition." Many people immediately connect the term "perdition" with hell and Judas with the devil. We have already seen that Judas was not the devil, but that he exhibited the devil's characteristics of slander and spite.

The word "perdition" may include hell and hell may include perdition, but they are distinct in meaning and different in application in many respects.

The word "perdition" is translated from the Greek word *apoleia,* meaning "ruin or loss." This could mean spiritual ruin or loss as well as eternal ruin or loss. It can also mean "damnable (damnation), destruction, die, perish, pernicious ways or waste." Hell is eternal; perdition is not always used in an eternal sense. Hebrews 10:39 contains a prime example of this:

> "But we are not of them who draw back unto perdition; but of them that believe to the saving of the soul" (Hebrews 10:39).

The writer of Hebrews is speaking to followers of Christ who were/are illuminated by the Gospel and sanctified, yet warns of drawing back into perdition, that is, into a life of ruin and loss, a life of pernicious (hurtful, deadly) ways. Note that those of us who are followers of Christ did not ascend from hell when we were born again (saved), but we were found on a wasteful, destructive path leading to hell. The perdition referred to in Hebrews 10:39 is not necessarily eternal, but it does carry a warning of returning to a sinful lifestyle.

Judas did draw back into a lifestyle of ruin and destruction. He fell by transgression. He would not have had to fall by transgression if he were already a devil or a "son of perdition." Therefore we see that it was the spiritual path that Judas took that caused him to become a "son of perdition" or a "son of ruin and loss." The decisions we make concerning morality do make a difference. Judas became a "son," an off-spring, of spiritual ruin or loss.

His Own Place

It is also said of Judas that he "went to his own place." This statement refers to the choices Judas made. The place that he went to after death was of his own choosing. He was the "son of perdition," without a chance of repentance, only because he took his own life. Was his fate "eternal perdition," that is, hell? Matthew Henry says this:

> "...the place of a traitor, the fittest place for him, not only to the gibbet, but to hell — this was his own place. Note, Those that betray Christ, as they fall from the dignity of relation to him, so they fall into all misery. It is said of Balaam (Num. 24:25) that he went to his own place, that is, says one of the rabbin, he went to hell. Dr. Whitby quotes Ignatius saying, There is appointed to every man *idios topos* — a proper place, which imports the same with that of God's rendering to every man according to his works. And our Saviour had said that Judas's own place should be such that it had been better for him that he had never been born (Mt. 26:24) — his misery such as to be worse than not being. Judas had been a hypocrite, and hell is the proper place of such; other sinners,

as inmates have their portion with them" (Mt. 24:51).

Godly Subjection

Hebrews 10:26 says the following concerning New Testament saints:

> "For if we sin wilfully after that we have received the knowledge of the truth, there remaineth no more sacrifice for sins...Of how much sorer punishment, suppose ye, shall he be thought worthy, who hath trodden under foot the Son of God, and hath counted the blood of the covenant, wherewith he was sanctified, an unholy thing, and hath done despite unto the Spirit of grace?" (Hebrews 10:26–29).

It is imperative that we follow Christ and bring our bodies into subjection as did the Apostle Paul (I Cor. 9:27). If we sin, we must sincerely confess our sins to God in Jesus' name. John wrote that He is faithful to forgive us and cleanse us from all sin.

> "Ye therefore, beloved, seeing ye know these things before, beware lest ye also, being led away with the error of the wicked, fall from your own stedfastness" (II Peter 3:17).

Whether we like it or not, we are caught up in the midst of spiritual warfare between right and wrong (Eph. 6:12). Therefore, the battles that often rage within us — whether thoughts of suicide or some other struggle — are spiritual and can only be resolved through spiritual means. Suicide is not an end. Suicide only kills the body. The soul and spirit continue to exist.

As stated earlier, we are not our own; we belong to God. It's not our right to take a life that doesn't belong to us. It's not our life; only the choices are ours. To murder oneself is to rob God of the purpose for which that life was created.

Scripture reveals that to take your own life stands in direct opposition to righteousness. We are told in Revelation 21:8 that murderers will be cast into the lake of fire (hell). The last act of a suicide victim is murder.

Those who commit suicide are not trusting God for the outcome of their life situations. They have nurtured thoughts in direct opposition to God. Judas by transgression (opposition to God) fell. Christians are severely warned against such falling. Note what Peter wrote in his second letter:

"For if after they have escaped the pollutions of the world through the knowledge of the Lord and Saviour Jesus Christ, they are again entangled therein, and overcome, the latter end is worse with them than the beginning (Judas was told this — Mrk. 14:21). For it had been better for them not to have known the way of righteousness, than, after they have known it, to turn from the holy commandment delivered unto them. But it is happened unto them according to the true proverb, The dog is turned to his own vomit again; and the sow that was washed to her wallowing in the mire" (II Peter 2:20–22) (parenthesis for clarification).

Is suicide wrong? Yes. Do **all** suicide victims go to hell? I don't know. Only God knows the circumstances surrounding each individual case. Thanks be to God that I am not the judge over the souls of men. Do most suicide victims go to hell? According to all the evidences given in God's Word, I would say yes.

If you are considering suicide, you had better think twice, three times, or as many times as it takes to convince yourself of who really owns you. You have been purchased by God (I Cor. 6:20); you are of great worth to Him (Jn. 3:16–17). Please know that Jesus can turn your life around and make you a new creature (II Cor. 5:17).

Hope and Help

Know that there is hope.

Here's how to get things on track:

1. Realize your situation (Rom. 3:10).
2. Know that all are sinners (Rom. 3:23).
3. Find the reason all are sinners (Rom. 5:12).
4. See the result of being a sinner (Rom. 6:23).
5. Know God's concern for sinners (Rom. 5:8).
6. Follow God's way of salvation (Rom. 10:9,10,13).

You can accept Jesus anywhere. You don't have to come to the Lord at a church service. I gave my heart to the Lord in the back floor-board of a 1959 Cadillac. After turning to the Lord for salvation, find a Bible-believing church (Heb. 10:25), be baptized (Acts 2:41), and continue to follow the teachings of Jesus (Matt. 16:24). Ω

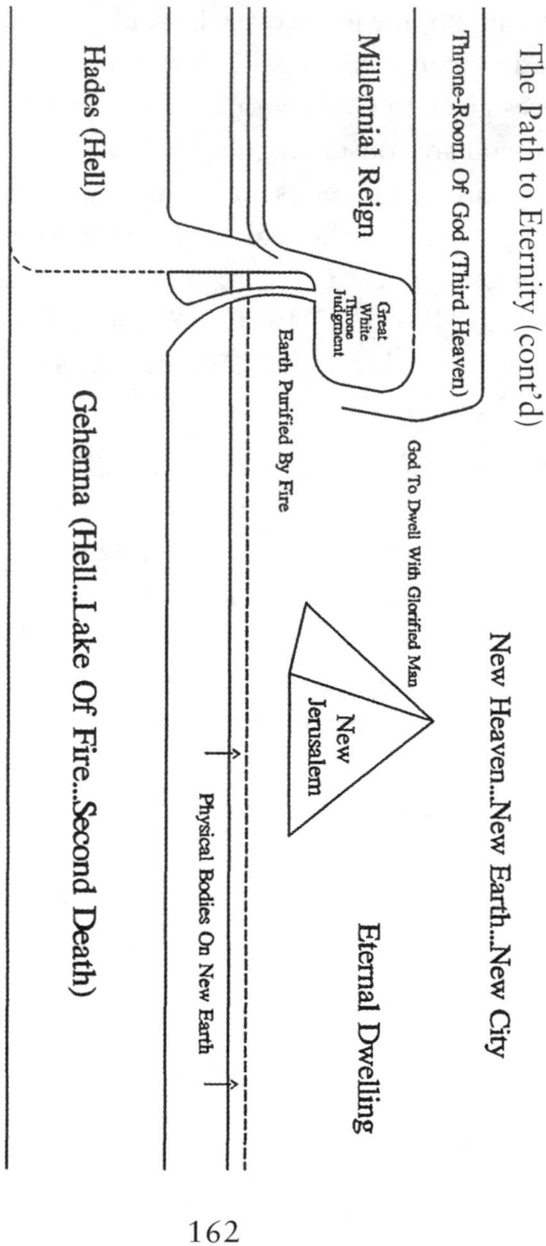

Continued from page 130

Charts by J.A.H.

CHAPTER
8

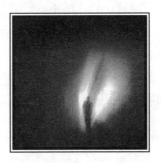

THE DEATH
OF A CHILD

Love is so powerful, it often comes in small
packages and for brief periods of time.

A very sad fact of life is that children die. They do not die because they are sinful. They die because they were born under the curse of sin and death brought on by the fall of Adam (Rom. 5:12).

The results of Adam's sin have also culminated in many terrible acts against innocent children. Today we hear of parents who drown them, allow them to suffocate in extreme temperatures while locked inside automobiles, beat them, molest them and shoot them to death. Children are abducted from homes and playgrounds to be tortured and sexually abused. Those who survive such horrors are left scarred for life.

The world is greatly plagued by people who have no regard for the lives of children. Just about any form of cruelty imaginable has been used against children. The thought of such things is saddening, yet they are not a new phenomenon. History is full of such horrendous acts.

We read in Scripture that children were systematically sacrificed by pagans. They were cast into pits of fire as an act of worship to their gods (Deut. 12:31; II Chron. 28:1; Jer. 7:30–31). Approximately two years after Jesus was born, King Herod ordered the murder of all children under the age of two in and around Bethlehem (Matt. 2:11,16). It is the innocent who always suffer when ignorance prevails.

Satan's plan always has been to thwart God's plan.

One such attack comes in the form of cruelty against the innocent. As a result, questions have been spawned about God's care and intent where children are concerned.

The fate of abused children does not go unnoticed by our Lord. Every thought and deed will be brought before God and every person will be judged, not only for how he or she treats children, but also how adults treat one another (Psa. 94:11; Matt 9:4; Rom. 13:2; Heb. 10:30–31). In John 12:48, Christ relates that those who reject Him and His words will be judged on the last day. Paul also expresses this importance in Romans 2:16, where he wrote that a day will come when God judges the secrets of men by Jesus Christ according to the Gospel. Every act against children, even those carried out in secret, will be dealt with; the guilty will not be forgotten. "Vengeance is mine; I will repay, saith the Lord" (Rom. 12:19).

Don't be fooled by the wiles of the devil. The Bible teaches that the Lord cares greatly for children. He paid special attention to them during His ministry and gave stern warnings against mistreating them.

> "...whoso shall receive one such little child in my name receiveth me. But whoso shall offend one of these little ones which believe in me, it were better for him that a millstone were hanged about his neck, and that he were drowned in the depth of the sea" (Matthew 18:5–6).

The word "offend" comes from the Greek word

skandalizo, which means "scandalize." To scandalize someone means to treat that person in a disgraceful or discreditable manner. It also means to give occasion to stumble or trip up. It's very simple: we cannot be cruel or disrespectful to children, nor should our actions cause occasion for a child to sin. Jesus continued:

> "Take heed that ye despise not one of these little ones; for I say unto you, That in heaven their angels do always behold the face of my Father which is in heaven" (Matthew 18:10).

The Greek word for "despise" is *kataphroneo,* which means to think against or disesteem. The mistreatment of a child is a most serious offense. We should not think for one moment that God is unaware of our actions toward children, for "their angels" are in constant contact with Him.

The above statements do not mean that we are to let children run wild without discipline (Prov. 1:7–8; 4:1; 22:6; 22:15), but that we are to love them, properly instruct them, and encourage them to do what is right and just toward God and man. Take time for children!

Jesus always took time for children and placed great emphasis on the characteristics of these little ones. In Matthew 19:13, Jesus' followers were bringing children to Him that He might touch them and bless them. The disciples rebuked the people for their actions. However, Jesus was very displeased with the disciples' actions and witness before these parents and their children. He instructed the disciples, "...forbid them not to come unto me."

Receiving the Kingdom

Moreover, we know that children are greatly favored by God, for "of such" is the kingdom of God (Matt. 19:14; Mrk. 10:14; Lk. 18:16). Jesus made it clear that individuals must receive the kingdom of God as little children or they cannot enter (Mrk. 10:15). That's a strong statement from our Lord. Luke put it this way:

> "Verily I say unto you, Whosoever shall not receive the king-dom of God as a little child shall in no wise enter therein" (Luke 18:17).

Here Luke records Jesus as saying that there is "no way" for a person to enter the kingdom of God except he comes to God as a little child. This does not mean that a person must be young to come to God, but that he must have the characteristics of a little child — whatever his or her age may be. A child begins life as dependent, responsive, submissive, obedient, ever-learning, humble and forgiving.

> "Whosoever therefore shall humble himself as this little child, the same is greatest in the kingdom of heaven" (Matthew 18:4).

Child Salvation

The death of a child raises many questions about his or her standing and destination. We know that a prerequisite for salvation is belief, right? We also know that Jesus died for all who would accept Him. But a child is too young to believe and too immature to consider the things around him so that he might believe. Does this mean that a child who dies is lost without hope? Absolutely not!

A child starts life pure and clean. Although born under the curse of death, children are without spiritual corruption or spiritual fault. And, as we have seen, Jesus placed great emphasis on the purity and innocence of children. Therefore God will not let the innocent perish without hope. However, we must realize that children will not be in heaven because they have pure and humble beginnings. Neither will they be in heaven because they have no spiritual fault.

Children go to heaven because God has accredited their sin nature to Christ. The reason is that they have not yet reached an age when they are able to determine a heartfelt belief in God. They are considered among those who "...have not the law, but are a law unto themselves" as are the "natives of the bush" mentioned in Romans 2:14;5:12. They are innocent and pure only because of God's mercy toward those who are unable to believe, whether through involuntary ignorance, mental incapability, or youth.

Age of Accountability

Of course we cannot know or even attempt to determine the age that a child becomes aware of his or her sin nature. It is impossible to know. Each child's mental development and mental capacity varies according to many factors. Each child differs according to what he or she has been taught, to his or her perception of his or her surroundings, and to his or her ability to reason. Some children are more mentally mature at a very young age while others are not. Due to disease or some other unfortunate mishap, some remain with the mental capacity of a small child throughout their lives. Children do not fit a particular mold for accountability.

Although God knows each of us better than we know ourselves, only the individual child knows when he or she is aware of doing good or bad and when he or she feels convicted of such. The judgment call is not ours.

A great responsibility is laid upon all parents to teach their children the difference between right and wrong. There is a shortage of this today. Many parents have preconceived notions and "individual truths" apart from God's will and plan. This is serious.

"Trust in the LORD with all thine heart; and lean not unto thine own understanding" (Proverbs 3:5).

"Train up a child in the way he should go: and when he is old, he will not depart from it" (Proverbs 22:6).

We must not turn a child away from the altar of salvation. We cannot judge those things that God is working in that life. King Josiah was eight years old when he began his reign in Jerusalem and did that which was right and good in the sight of the Lord (II Kings 22:1–2). Josiah apparently was blessed with God-fearing advisors who despised the idolatrous influence of his father, Amon. Josiah apparently believed in and trusted God very early in his life. As a result of Josiah's trust, the Lord dealt with his heart mightily. Around the age of sixteen, he more deeply sought out the God of David (II Chron. 34:3). As a result of his seeking the Lord, he started to cleanse the land of idolatry at the age of twenty (II Chron. 34:3–7).

We do not know and cannot know what the Lord has in store for children who come to Him. We must "forbid them not" because God may be calling them to be a "Josiah."

We cannot judge whether the child who dies having lived only a few years was yet aware of things right or wrong. I do know that it is a serious matter to lead a child into sin or teach him or her things contrary to the plan of God (Matt. 18:6). I do believe that only God and the child can know the appropriate age that one is called by the Spirit and becomes accountable. Those who are incapable of choosing for themselves will not perish, for God is just.

He Took a Child

Great care should be taken when dealing with children. Not only do we shape and mold their lives by our actions, but we also form a witness before God and man. This is very important in the eyes of the Lord. How we treat children is a very good indicator of how we treat others. Jesus gave an example of this, as recorded in Mark 9:33–37.

The disciples were arguing among themselves about who would be greatest in the kingdom. Jesus said, "If any man desire to be first, the same shall be last of all, servant of all." Jesus then revealed the heart of a servant. He took a child in his arms and started to teach, immediately revealing His care and concern for children. Note that He did not grab or snatch up a child, but "took a child," a tender, caring action. He was revealing that we are to serve others in order to be great in the kingdom.

In word and deed Jesus expressed that the very qualities needed to take up a child are the same qualities it takes to become a servant to others. With care and concern, we are to use courage to reach them, humility to convince them, faith to compel them, patience to encourage them and a forgiving heart to comfort them. We are to use love to reveal Christ to the world as we would love and care for a child.

Blaming God

Some see the death of a child as mockery. It is as though God is taking a life before he or she really begins to live or experience the joy of accomplishment.

Because of this, many who lose a child to death blame God for their loss. We must not blame God, for it is God who takes the child and caresses him or her in His arms. He takes care of them much better than we ever could. In fact, we do not know what children have been spared by what appears to be untimely deaths.

If anyone is to blame for the death of a child, it's the devil. The devil's deceptive tactics caused Eve to partake of the forbidden fruit. Or, if we must blame someone, we might blame Adam for not straightening the whole mess out rather then partaking of the forbidden fruit when Eve offered it to him. Noting, of course, that God made Adam the person responsible for the direction and care for both Eve and himself. Because Adam did not take charge of the situation, he brought sin and death upon himself, upon Eve, and upon all of mankind (Rom. 5:12). This fate included the suffering and mistreatment of children.

A recitation by famed bass singer, J.D. Sumner, goes something like this:

"I was walkin' in Savannah past a church decayed and dim
there slowly through the window came a plantiff funeral hymn
and a sympathy awakened and a wonder quickly grew until
I found myself environed in a little negro pew
Down front set a young couple in sorrow nearly wild
on the altar lay a coffin, in the coffin lay a child
Rose a sad old negro preacher at a little wooden desk with

a manner grandly offered and a countenance grotesque
And he said, Now don't be a weepin' for dis pretty bit of clay
For the little boy what lived da, he done gone and run away
He's doin' veri finely an he preciates ya love,
But he sho'nough farther roamin' in dat lage house up above
Now He didn't give you dat baby, not by a hundud tousand miles
He just think you need some sunshine an He lent'em fo a while
An he letcha love and keep'im til yo hearts was bigger grown
An dem silver tears yo sheddin' they jest interest on da loan
So my poor dejected mourners, letcha hearts with Jesus rest
An don't go critizin' da One dat knows da best
He's done give us many comforts and He has a right to take away
To da Lawd be praise and glory, now and forever, let us pray."
(TRADITIONAL)

Abortion

The definition of the word "abort" is "to fail, cease, or stop at an early or premature stage." Today the term "fail" certainly fits where human life is concerned. Often, there is a physical or medical reason why the unborn are miscarried. This is called a "spontaneous abortion," an unplanned and unsolicited loss of the unborn. However, premeditated abortion is quite another matter. It is the deliberate murder of the unborn child. Although in some cultures it is an acceptable way to end an unplanned pregnancy, it is still the murder of an innocent life and is an action with sin written all over it.

Many try to avoid the obvious and avert the truth by questioning "what ifs" and "could-have-beens." We debate whether life truly begins at conception and whether the tissue is actually a human life until the "fetus" is several weeks old. As we will see, Scripture quickly puts the issue of induced abortion in its proper place.

God's Gift

Children are important to God even before they are born. In Genesis 18:9–15 God told Abraham that his barren wife Sarah would have a son. He kept His promise in that Sarah conceived and bore Abraham a son (Gen. 21:1–2). Rebekah was also barren, yet Isaac prayed and she conceived (Gen. 25:21). This was also the case with Leah (Gen. 29:31–35); Rachel (Gen. 30:22–23); and Hannah (I Sam. 1:19–20).

In the New Testament, the birth of John the Baptist was a miracle given to a "childless couple" (Lk. 1:13). This was the fulfillment of an Old Testament prophecy (Isa. 40:3). Before she even had sexual relations with any man, Mary was promised that she would bear Jesus (Lk. 1:26–38). This, too, was a fulfillment of prophecy (Isa. 9:6). She was still a virgin when Christ was born (Matt. 1:23–25). These cases reveal that conception is God's intention for birth and it is God's gift.

We read in earlier chapters that our life is not our own and that we have no right to take it — not our life, not anyone else's life, not even the life of the unborn. Many people treat the unborn as only waste to be discarded. But the life conceived in the womb is not ours to dispose of; that life also belongs to God.

Job said:

> "Did not he that made me in the womb make him? and did not one fashion us in the womb?" (Job 31:15).

Jeremiah, a prophet of God, relates to us that even before we are conceived in the womb God knows who we are:

> "Before I formed thee in the belly I knew thee; and before thou camest forth out of the womb I sanctified thee, and I ordained thee a prophet unto the nations" (Jeremiah 1:5).

Here we are told that it is the Lord who created man, forms infants in the womb, and directs our path (Isa. 45:12–13). As seen in earlier chapters, we belong to God.

In conjunction with Mary's foretold conception, Jesus was also named before He was conceived of the Holy Ghost (Matt. 1:18; Lk. 1:31):

> "And when eight days were accomplished for the circumcising of the child, his name was called JESUS, **which was so named of the angel before he was conceived in the womb**" (Luke 2:21).

Playing God

For man to take a life from the womb is to play God and actually rob God of His creation. It's very simple: induced abortion is murder. The psalmist made it clear when he wrote about those who commit such iniquity:

> "They slay the widow and the stranger, and murder the

fatherless (child). Yet they say, The LORD shall not see, neither shall the God of Jacob regard it. Understand, ye brutish
among the people: and ye fools, when will ye be wise?.... The
LORD knoweth the thoughts of man, that they are vanity"
(Psalm 94:6–7,11).

Abortion Biblical?

Many so-called Christians and abortion advocates
try to support their stance by using verses in the Bible.
This is accomplished through the use of incorrectly
translated versions of Scripture. One of the main passages of Scripture that they use to base their argument
is Exodus 21:22–25. It is said that an unborn child's
life is not as important as one who has been born due
to the penalty that is given. The penalty for killing a
child who has been born is death, while the death of
an unborn child only carries a fine. However, this is
not what Scripture says. Exodus 21:22–25 actually
says:

> "If men strive, and hurt a woman with child, so that her fruit
> depart from her, and yet no mischief follow: he shall be
> surely punished, according as the woman's husband will lay
> upon him; and he shall pay as the judges determine. And if
> any mischief follow, then thou shalt give life for life, Eye for
> eye, tooth for tooth, hand for hand, foot for foot, Burning
> for burning, wound for wound, stripe for stripe" (Exodus
> 21:22–25).

Pro-choice proponents use the term "miscarriage" in the place of "her fruit depart" and add that
only a fine was prescribed for the miscarriage. Again,

these terms are from "new" versions of the Bible. The term "miscarriage" is used here as losing the unborn child to death. However, the word "fruit," from the Hebrew word *yeled* is used here. It means, "something born, a lad or offspring." The word for "depart" is *yatsa,* which means "appear, break out, bring forth, escape, issue out," and so on. This reference does not include miscarriage in the Hebrew or anywhere else. The King James translation more accurately describes the proper definition of *yeled yatsa* as "fruit depart." What *yeled yatsa* means is that the child was born prematurely due to the misguided blow by one of the men. This is further substantiated by the phrase "...and yet no mischief follow." In other words if neither the child nor the woman dies, only a fine may be administered for the premature birth and for any problems that may follow. However, if mischief (*acown* — hurt) does occur (the woman or the child dies as a result of the blow) a life for a life is required. An eye for an eye and a tooth for a tooth, et cetera. That is, the penalty for killing the child (unborn or born) or the woman was death.

Jesus did not void this approach in Matthew 5:38–42. Certainly we are to be patient with our fellow man, turn the other cheek and so forth. However, Jesus first said, "That ye resist not evil." We are not to let evil take over, nor are we to seek evil for evil. He was quoting Exodus as an example for us not to bear a grudge or resent those who have wronged us. A Christian is not to be a revengeful person. The point of the matter in Exodus 21:22–25 is that life is precious, even for the unborn. If that life was taken in death, the penalty for taking that life was death.

Life Begins at Conception

"But thou art he that took me out of the womb: thou didst make me hope when I was upon my mother's breasts. I was cast upon thee from the womb: thou art my God from my mother's belly" (Psalm 22:9–10).

"For thou hast possessed my reins: thou hast covered me in my mother's womb. I will praise thee; for I am fearfully and wonderfully made: marvellous are thy works; and that my soul knoweth right well. My substance was not hid from thee, when I was made in secret, and curiously wrought in the lowest parts of the earth. Thine eyes did see my substance, yet being unperfect; and in thy book all my members were written, which in continuance were fashioned, when as yet there was none of them" (Psalm 139:13–16).

"Thus saith the LORD that made thee, and formed thee from the womb, which will help thee; Fear not, O Jacob, my servant; and thou, Jesurun, whom I have chosen" (Isaiah 44:2).

"Thus saith the LORD, thy redeemer, and he that formed thee from the womb, I am the LORD that maketh all things; that stretcheth forth the heavens alone; that spreadeth abroad the earth by myself;..." (Isaiah 44:24).

"Listen, O isles, unto me; and hearken, ye people, from far; The LORD hath called me from the womb; from the bowels of my mother hath he made mention of my name. And he hath made my mouth like a sharp sword; in the shadow of his hand hath he hid me, and made me a polished shaft; in his quiver hath he hid me; And said unto me, Thou art my servant, O Israel, in whom I will be glorified. Then I said, I have laboured in vain, I have spent my strength for nought, and in vain: yet surely my judgment is with the LORD, and my work with my God. And now, saith the LORD that formed me from the womb to be his servant, to bring Jacob again to him, Though Israel be not gathered, yet shall I be glorious in the eyes of the LORD, and my God shall be my strength" (Isaiah 49:1-5).

"Did not he that made me in the womb make him? and did not one fashion us in the womb?" (Job 31:15).

"Before I formed thee in the belly I knew thee; and before thou camest forth out of the womb I sanctified thee, and I ordained thee a prophet unto the nations" (Jeremiah 1:5).

"And it came to pass, that, when Elisabeth heard the salutation of Mary, the babe leaped in her womb; and Elisabeth was filled with the Holy Ghost:..." (Luke 1:41).

Forgiveness

There is forgiveness for those who have performed abortions, for those who promote abortions and for those who have had abortions. Jesus taught this in Matthew 5:38-42. Thanks be to God for the plan of escape for our wicked and sinful nature:

"If we confess our sins, he is faithful and just to forgive us our sins, and to cleanse us from all unrighteousness. If we say that we have not sinned, we make him a liar, and his word is not in us. My little children, these things write I unto you, that ye sin not. And if any man sin, we have an advocate with the Father, Jesus Christ the righteous: And he is the propitiation for our sins: and not for ours only, but also for the sins of the whole world" (I John 1:9-2:2).

Perspective

I saw a bumper sticker as I was driving that read, "It seems hypocritical to vote for abortion after you've already been born."

Yes, children who die, die with the grace of God upon them whatever the means of their death. They will be found in the arms of God, who is a loving and caring Father. For those who are still children and for those who have not been born, it's our duty as parents and grandparents to train these little ones in the ways of the Lord:

"And, ye fathers, provoke not your children to wrath: but bring them up in the nurture and admonition of the Lord" (Ephesians 6:4).

As Abel's blood cried out from the ground, so does the blood of the innocent for the judgment of God—and judgment will be given.

"So ye shall not pollute the land wherein ye are: for blood it defileth the land: and the land cannot be cleansed of the blood that is shed therein, but by the blood of him that shed it" (Numbers 35:33). Ω

CHAPTER
9

CONCERNING LAST THINGS: CREMATION OR BURIAL

When death comes we leave behind us all that
we have and take with us all that we are.

181

Ashes to Ashes, Dust to Dust

I have heard this phrase all of my life; however, it is not found in Scripture. It is true that man came from dust (Gen. 2:7). It is true that man will return to dust (Gen. 3:19). The Bible teaches that from dust we came and to dust we shall return. But this is not said of ashes returning to ashes.

When Abraham said that he was but dust and ashes, he was speaking of his humility. He had taken upon himself to speak to the Lord on behalf of the righteous who were living in Sodom. Speaking of himself, Abraham said, "...which am but dust" (*'aphar* — clay, earth, mud), and ashes (*'epher* — to bestrew or scatter about).

> "And Abraham answered and said, Behold now, I have taken upon me to speak unto the Lord, **which am but dust and ashes**: Peradventure there shall lack five of the fifty righteous: wilt thou destroy all the city for lack of five? And he said, If I find there forty and five, I will not destroy it" (Genesis 18:27-28).

Job displayed the same type of humility as he went through his test of faith (Job 30:19). Note that while the words of both Abraham and Job were spoken, Abraham and Job were yet alive. In their estimation, they considered themselves nothing more than scattered clay.

The word "ashes" occurs in Scripture approximately 43 times, but never refers to man's return to ashes. It is mentioned only one time in connection with man's body and this is referring to his remembrances or memorials while in wickedness. Even this instance supplies separation between the remembrances of the body and the body of clay (Job 13:12). With all this said, we must ask: Is cremation an acceptable and proper mode of disposal for the human body?

Cremation

The word "cremate" simply means to reduce to ashes by fire, especially as a funeral rite. Cremation is becoming more and more popular in the Western world due to over-crowded cemeteries, the cost of burials and the influx of Eastern thought and secular humanism. The resulting belief system of secular humanism is that man is not accountable to God. It is but a part of an "all-is-one" theology that expresses that man is his own god and is accountable to no one but himself.

Cremation has been around for thousands of years. It is a practice that has separated Jews and Christians from other religions and customs of the world. Why? It has to do with the degree of respect with which each religious group or custom regards the human body.

As we read in Chapter Two, Christians (as well as Jews) realize that man is made in the image of Almighty God. Moreover, Christians and Jews are instructed through Scripture to separate from the religious practices of paganism. Although very few individuals even consider the paganistic aspect of cremation, it has been a practice among pagans for thousands of years.

Cremation was practiced among the Babylonians, the Greeks and the Romans, all of whom were pagan (polytheistic) in their religious beliefs and practices. The Romans often cremated their dead and deposited their ashes in ornate funeral urns. Cremation is also practiced today, almost exclusively among the Hindus of India.

Fire Offering

Burning the human body is closely related to the respect given to fire above the respect given to the human body. Fire was a means by which the gods were paid homage. The ultimate homage being paid was in honoring the gods by burning the human body. Fire was an intricate part of many cultures of the ancient world. The Canaanites sacrificed their children on flaming altars (Deut. 12:31). Although God's people of the Old Testament used fire to offer animal sacrifices, they were warned that the practice of the heathen was an abomination to Him and should be avoided (Ezek. 16:20-21; II Chr. 28:3). Of course, this was not only because of the fire worship, but because of the manner in which the worship of other gods was administered through fire. However, very few people today consider worship of any kind, much less cremation, as a religious practice.

Modern Cremation

Obviously the act of cremation involves flames of fire or intense heat. Modern technology has supplied a process of heat that reaches some 2,500 degrees Fahrenheit by which bodies are disposed. This is accomplished by using cracked petroleum or gas directly applied to the body. In only a short period of time the body is reduced to ashes and bone fragments. Remaining bone fragments are removed from the ashes, pulverized and placed into a cremation urn.

Biblical Cremation

Although the English word "cremation" is not found in the Bible, it is found under different words and phrases in the Hebrew and Greek from which the English Bible was translated. For instance, the word *serephah* is found approximately 12 times in Scripture. *Serephah* refers to either the burning of a sacrifice, judgment from the Lord, or the disposal of unwanted goods. *Caraph* is used only one time in the Hebrew and supplies an hypothesis of 10 men who escape from the enemy, yet, they all die as a result of sickness. An uncle or next of kin may dispose of the bodies by fire. The burning of these bodies was acceptable in order to avoid the spread of disease. The reference also reveals the unbelieving status of the victims. The men were found in folly by not first calling upon God or even mentioning His name (Amos 6:10).

Another Hebrew word for "cremation" is *misraphah*. It is used in Isaiah 33:12 as a metaphor, not the actual act of cremation. ("And the people shall be *as* the burnings [*misraphah*-cremation] of lime: *as* thorns cut up shall they be burned [*yatsath*-set on fire] in the fire ['*esh*-burning]"). This word is used one other time and concerns the death of Zedekiah and the "burnings of thy fathers" (Jer. 34:5). This refers to the burning of odors with which the bodies of kings and royalty were honored. It is the burning of spices as a funeral rite and does not include the actual burning of the body except in cases of emergency or disease.

The Burning of King Saul

Burning the body as a funeral rite was forbidden for the Hebrews except under the most unusual cases of emergency. One such situation was when King Saul and his sons were burnt with fire and their bones were buried (I Sam. 31:12).

Due to the hot climate of the area, interment followed death by only hours, not days. However, this was not the case with Saul and his sons. After Saul had killed himself and his sons had died in battle, their bodies had lain on the battlefield for an entire day. It was not until the next day that the Philistines came to strip the dead (I Sam. 31:8) and found the bodies of Saul and his sons.

Saul's armor was then taken and hung on the wall in the temple of Ashtaroth, the Philistine goddess. Saul's severed head was sent around the Philistine camps and to the houses of their idols to boast about their victory (I Sam. 31:9). His body was hung on a wall in Bethshan. No doubt Saul's body was bloated, infested with insects, and very odorous. His body would have been beyond ointment and wrapping or any such care as was due kings. Moreover, as seen earlier, Saul's death was one without honor as well. The only feasible thing for the valiant men to do was to confiscate the body and dispose of it in the most expeditious manner: they burned it. The prolonged discovery of Saul's sons' bodies would also demand immediate disposal. This is one unusual case of emergency in which the Hebrews were allowed to burn their dead.

God's Cremation

In Scripture, the burning of individuals, idols and cities was the direct result of God's judgment upon sin. This burning was done to cleanse the land of diseases (Josh 7:25; 11:13; II Samuel 5:21; 23:6; II Kings 10:26; 23:6,11,15,16,20; I Chron. 14:12; Jer. 49:2; 51:58; Rev. 18:8). One such case is that of Achan, who had taken a Baylonish garment, 200 shekels of silver and a wedge of gold from the city of Jericho. The garment was to be burned with the city, and the silver and gold taken into the treasury. This burning was to

187

destroy the disease and illness, wickedness and corruption that was spawning in the city due to the sexual immorality that accompanied paganistic worship. Achan's sin was great because of his disobedience. In addition, he brought the threat of disease into the camp of Israel. Because of this, Achan, his family and their possessions were burned with fire (Josh. 7:20-25).

Revelations from God's Word express that burning the human body is linked to God's judgment upon sin. It is also strongly linked to paganism. The fact of the matter is, whether we recognize it as such or not, Christians are not to participate in pagan practices of any kind, especially when Christians are to be followers of Christ. The body of Christ was not burned, it was buried. This example should be sufficient in settling the matter.

Note: Cremation concerns the deliberate burning of the body and not accidental burning, as we will read about shortly.

Biblical Burial

When Abraham was called out of the pagan city of Ur and God spoke to him, He clearly commanded that Abraham would be buried:

> "And thou shalt go to thy fathers in peace; **thou shalt be buried** in a good old age" (Genesis 15:15) (see also Gen. 25:8,9).

In addition, God didn't burn Moses; He buried

Him:

> "So Moses the servant of the LORD died there in the land
> of Moab, according to the word of the LORD. **And he
> buried him** in a valley in the land of Moab, over against
> Bethpeor: but no man knoweth of his sepulchre unto this
> day" (Deuteronomy 34:5-6).

Burial among God's people is very prominent in
Scripture. Some burials recorded in Scripture are:
Abraham and Sarah (Gen. 49:31); Isaac and Rebekah
(Gen. 49:31); Leah (Gen. 49:31); Jacob (Gen. 47:28-
30); Rachel (Gen. 35:19-20); Rebekah's nurse (Gen.
35:8). The list could go on and on. Even in the New
Testament we find these burials: John the Baptist
(Matt. 14:8-12); Ananias and Sapphira (Acts 5:5-10);
and Christ Jesus (I Cor. 15:3-4). Moreover, the
believer's baptism is the likeness of Christ's death, **burial**, and resurrection (Rom. 6:4; Col. 2:12).

How much more should we be determined to follow the example of Christ in burial rather than in the
pagan practice of burning? It becomes very obvious
that the practice of the New Testament believer should
include burial rather than cremation.

Graves Opened

Graves opened when Jesus arose (Matt. 27:53) and
graves will burst open at the resurrection (Jn. 5:28).
There will be no grave to burst open if we are scattered
to the wind, to the water, or to the air.

"Marvel not at this: for the hour is coming, in the which all that are in the **graves** shall hear his voice,..." (John 5:28).

Martyrs have been burned at the stake, and saints have been accidentality consumed by fire, eaten by sharks, et cetera. Some Christians have died unaware of the paganistic, unscriptural nature of cremation. There are those who have not even considered the repulsiveness of burning the temple of God, the human body, as a funeral rite. Some Christians have been cast from ships or cast into vats of molten liquid. No doubt their bodily components will come together and will be resurrected in the last day. God is sovereign and is able to raise them up just as He is able to raise up stones (Matt. 3:9). But deliberate cremation is not proper for the Christian.

Cremation, by its very nature of consuming with fire or intense heat, conveys the connection and message of judgment and sin. God is love (I Jn. 4:8); however, our God is a consuming fire against the wicked (Ex. 24:17; Deut. 4:24; Heb. 12:29; Gen. 19:24; Lev. 10:1-2). Burning the human body by fire is found in Scripture as a judgment against sin and is the practice of those who oppose God. The fire of hell is an everlasting fire connected with judgment upon sin. The things with which the burning of the human body are connected reveal that cremation does not keep good company.

Scripturally, the graves, not the elements, are to burst open. Scripturally, the bodies in graves will arise.

The corruptible body of dust, not ashes, is referred to as "putting on incorruption." If I should die before the Rapture, I don't want an extra-biblical, paganistic form of burning my body. If I should die before the Rapture, I wish for my body to return to the dust from which it came. I want to follow the example of Christ, the example of Scripture and the example of those in Scripture who were followers of God both in the Old and New Testament.

"In the sweat of thy face shalt thou eat bread, till thou return unto the ground; for out of it wast thou taken: for dust thou art, and **unto dust shalt thou return**" (Genesis 3:19).

Cremation, exclusively, has no consequence on salvation, but it does have consequence on witness. The Apostle Paul desired that even if we die before the Lord's return, our entire being be preserved blameless (I Thess. 5:23). The preservation of the spirit and soul is in God's hands. He has left the preservation of the body to us along with the example of Scripture. Cremation maintains the stigma of paganism simply because it is not scriptural. Ω

-Note of Interest-
Baptism for the Dead

Paganism has supplied many false avenues of worship. One such fallacy is called the Baptism for the Dead. Paul mentioned this heathen practice while giving example of the resurrection (I Cor. 15:29). If there is no resurrection, then why do "they" (the heathen) practice such baptism?

Long before water baptism was commanded by Christ, baptism and other rituals on behalf of the dead already existed. There were those who cut their flesh, marked their bodies by tattooing or by shaving portions of their bodies for the dead (Lev. 19:28; 21:1-5; Deut. 14:1; I Kings 18:28; Jer. 16:7,16). These practices were used as a method to attract the attention of a particular god.

Baptism was a part of the ancient initiations of paganism. Many viewed the Flood as a type of baptismal regeneration. The ark represented the great egg that hatched new life. Although the descendants of the ancient mystery religions claim that Jesus was only affirming their practice, baptism was commanded by Jesus Christ in stark contrast to the pagan practice of baptism. Jesus proclaimed that believers are to be baptized in the name of the Father, the Son and the Holy Ghost. To do so was to reject the pagan forms of baptism and outwardly affirm one's belief in the death, burial and resurrection of Jesus.

> "Go ye therefore, and teach all nations, baptizing them in the name of the Father, and of the Son, and of the Holy Ghost: Teaching them to observe all things whatsoever I have commanded you: and, lo, I am with you alway, even unto the end of the world. Amen" (Matthew 28:19-20). Ω

CHAPTER
1 0

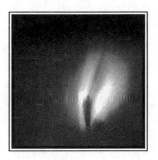

DECEPTION:
THE WALKING DEAD

An honest man alters his ideas to fit the
truth, and a dishonest man alters the truth to fit
his ideas. We lie loudest when we lie to ourselves.

The heart of man is prone to accept what is not of God. Many times the things our heart tells us are in stark contrast to God's plan and His will. Moreover, many such persuasions reach beyond personal deception. They extend into religious practice whereby others are deceived and doomed for eternity. This tactic has been used by Satan since his fall from heaven and is still in operation today. Persuading others to doubt God and to place our trust elsewhere is his deceptive tactic: "Hath God said?"

The very foundation of believing in Jesus as a living Savior lies in His resurrection (Rom. 10:9-10). It should come as no surprise that the arch enemy has contrived false resurrections in an attempt to falsify the true. One avenue of the master deceiver's work is found in the practice of the walking dead called zombies.

The Walking Dead

Voodoo is the prevailing system of religion in Haiti. Its origins are in Africa, especially in Benin (formerly Dahomey). In the Fon language of Africa, the term voodoo is "vodun," which means "god" or "spirit." It combines features of African and native West Indian religion with many Roman Catholic practices and beliefs, liturgistics and sacraments.

Voodoo combines a belief in one god (Bondye) with a belief in various kinds of spirits. It is believed that each individual is made up of several souls. These souls become spirits after the death of the individual. These spirits, in turn, may take possession of another individual. The outward expression of this is revealed through ritual dances, animal sacrifice for the spirit, counsel and advice. This is yet another form of religion apart from that intended by Creator God.

Beyond sacrifice and counsel, the spirit operates as guardian angel and patron saint. The purpose of voodoo is to serve these spirits and remain in good standing with them. *Bondye*, the voodoo god, is considered remote and unapproachable. As a result, real devotion is given to the spirits. These spirits, called *loa* or *lwa* in the Yoruba language, are not considered evil and serve as intermediaries between the people and *Bondye*, as is found in the Roman Catholic practice of prayers to saints.

The Resurrection

The voodoo deities or *loa* are closely related to African gods and may be revealed in the spirits of natural phenomena such as fire, water, wind or of the dead, including eminent ancestors.

As the main belief in one god is manifested by many spirits, the religion has many avenues of expression. One particular manifestation is the belief and practice of the resurrection of the dead. This is not a belief system based on the resurrection of Christ, but a belief in their own particular form of resurrection. This is due to the practice of *bocor,* the voodoo priest.

Zombies

The voodoo priest is especially dreaded for his supposed ability to create the zombie, a newly dead, soulless corpse that the priest reanimates (resurrects) by supposedly causing the dead body to be possessed by an elemental spirit under his control. The resurrected individual (zombie) moves about in a trance-like state and does the bidding of the priest. They are called the "walking dead." The term "zombie" is apparently derived from Nzambi, a West African deity.

The resurrection by the voodoo priest is a far cry from the resurrection of Christ. Although the spirits governing this practice are truly of the spirit world (demonic), research has found that it is nothing more than clever deceit. (For more on demons, see author's book, *The Unveiling*, pgs. 183 and 198.)

Voodoo Resurrection

Researchers have found that the voodoo priest chooses his victim by first causing the symptoms of death. Powder containing a powerful neurotoxin is secretly placed in the path of the chosen individual. The powder may be placed on a hand-tool, a window sill or wherever is deemed necessary to expose the victim. This neurotoxin comes from a fish called the "puffer fish." The powder allegedly paralyzes the victim into a deathlike state: a false death. The priest then examines the "corpse" to determine the amount of his exposure to the powder. An estimated time for the neurotoxin to wear off is made and thus a time is set for a "resurrection from the dead."

The victim is buried and then exhumed at the prescribed interval. Brain damage results from improper calculations. The victim may exist in a vegetative or trancelike state, largely due to lack of oxygen. Real death may also be the result. If proper calculations are made, the victim is resurrected and made useful for the priest's bidding. Such supposed proof of the priest's power brings the people into greater subjection to the priesthood and into a deeper commitment to a false religion. Here the truth is most definitely altered in order to fit a religious and selfish purpose. This is deception.

The Real Walking Dead

All we think, all we say, all we do and all we are should be in submission to God through the Holy Spirit. To submit to God through repentance of sin is known as salvation. If we do not yield to God, we remain in our sins. In reality, to live in such a state, is to be dead, spiritually dead. Scripture makes it quite clear that we were considered dead in the trespasses of our sins before we came to Christ:

> "And you hath he quickened, who were dead in trespasses and sins: Wherein in time past ye walked according to the course of this world, according to the prince of the power of the air, the spirit that now worketh in the children of disobedience:...Even when we were dead in sins, hath quickened us together with Christ, (by grace ye are saved;)..."

(Ephesians 2:1,2,5).

These verses reveal the real walking dead. They are physically alive, yet they are dead. The life-force within functions according to the natural man, but in reality, they are dead. Such individuals go about the daily routine of acting out decisions, eating, drinking and experiencing life, but they are dead. The true condition of such individuals is as that of the hypocritical religious leaders of Jesus' day. They were those who denied the truth. Scripture reveals that they were full of dead men's bones:

> "Woe unto you, scribes and Pharisees, hypocrites! for ye are like unto whited sepulchres, which indeed appear beautiful outward, **but are within full of dead men's bones**, and of all uncleanness" (Matthew 23:27).

Truly Walking Dead

In the book of Luke (9:59-60) a man wished to follow Christ; however, he first desired to bury his father. Jesus wanted the man to trust Him and begin right away to proclaim the kingdom of God. Jesus said, "Let the dead bury their dead." How do dead men bury dead men? The only possible way is for a spiritually dead man to bury a physically dead man. Although this man's request was that he be given the opportunity to wait until his father died before he submitted to Christ, we see by this statement that there is such a thing as a walking dead man.

It is imperative that a spiritual resurrection occur for the spiritually dead man. This resurrection can only come through Jesus Christ:

> "Who his own self bare our sins in his own body on the tree, that we, being dead to sins, should live unto righteousness: by whose stripes ye were healed" (I Peter 2:24).

Coming to Christ makes one a new creature, a creature truly and spiritually alive. All things become new (II Cor. 5:17). Simply changing our attitudes or filling our lives with good intentions will not work. We must confess with our mouths the Lord Jesus and believe in His bodily resurrection (Rom. 10:9-10). We are then to follow Him through His Word. We are to be crucified with Christ (Rom. 6:6). It is the crucifying of the old man and the giving of our lives fully to Christ that resurrects from the dead:

> "Neither yield ye your members as instruments of unrighteousness unto sin: but yield yourselves unto God, **as those that are alive from the dead,** and your members as instruments of righteousness unto God" (Romans 6:13).

> "Therefore, brethren, we are debtors, not to the flesh, to live after the flesh. For if ye live after the flesh, ye shall die: but if ye through the Spirit do mortify the deeds of the body, ye shall live" (Romans 8:12-13).

If the Lord tarries, then all who are presently living will physically die and another generation will take our place. It is both honorable and precious to God for those who die prepared:

"Precious in the sight of the LORD is the death of his saints" (Psalm 116:15).

Death becomes precious to the Lord because those who die IN the Lord experience the long-awaited transition into eternal life. It will be eternal death for those who die without accepting the plan of eternal life. God has no pleasure in the death of those who die, those who have not had a spiritual resurrection:

"For I have no pleasure in the death of him that dieth, saith the Lord GOD: wherefore turn yourselves, and live ye" (Ezekiel 18:32).

Near Death — Bright Light

If you, like the voodoo priest, are spiritually dead, you are walking in deception, self-deception. We have seen earlier that we cannot trust what our hearts tell us, or what appears to be (Jn. 7:24); we must trust God and what He has said in His Word.

There are those who have had near-death experiences who felt such a peace and comfort, yet who have never trusted the Lord Jesus for salvation. The fear of death is often removed and a peace comes into their lives. The experience changes their outlook on life, but for the most part, they remain unbelievers in Christ Jesus. The near-death experience leaves them so comforted that they feel no need for a Savior. Many experience the spiritual visual of a "bright light." We must remember that near-death experiences are just that,

"NEAR death." Thus, we are still subject to deception. It just might be something or someone other than God revealing a drawing light and semblance of peace:

"And no marvel; for Satan himself is transformed into an angel of light" (II Corinthians 11:14).

Experiencing a "bright light" does not extinguish the need for salvation. Although many Christians have experienced a similar "bright light," we cannot base our belief system on experience or feelings. We walk by faith. We must also be aware of the wiles of the devil.

Some people have had out-of-body experiences who seemingly floated above the death occurrence only to be brought back by modern technology or the expertise of a bystander. These, too, are near-death experiences. It is a time when the body, soul and spirit begin separating, yet the appointment of physical death is postponed. The body fails life, but is brought back from physical death to life.

We have discussed in previous chapters how the body, soul, and spirit separate at death. In the brief moments of this separation, the soul, with all of its awareness, feelings and emotion, leaves the body. Therefore it is possible to have an out-of-body experience. Speaking of himself, the Apostle Paul expressed his viewing the third heaven as a possible "out-of-body" experience (II Cor. 12:2-3). Whatever the case, it was a very real experience expressing a real place.

We can trust this experience from Paul because he lived a scriptural, dedicated, godly life as a Christian.

The prophet Elijah (through God) raised the son of the Zarephath widow (I Kings 17:20-24). He cried out to the Lord that the boy's soul return to his body that he might live again. The Lord heard the man of God and the boy's soul returned, hence, life re-entered the boy's body. Again, there is such a thing as the separation of the body, soul and spirit, as we saw in Chapters Two and Three. The fact is, we cannot trust what occurs between the brief period of death and destination. We must not build philosophies and doctrines for life based on experience apart from salvation in Christ Jesus. "Marvel not that I said unto thee, Ye must be born again."

God's Word also says that there is an appointment for death. With the exception of Enoch (Gen. 6:9; Heb. 11:5), Elijah (II Kings 2:1-11), and those who are alive at the Rapture (I Cor. 15:51-53; I Thess. 4: 13-18), death is coming. It is not something we gladly welcome because of our nature. Instead, it is a grim reminder of our mortality. Death is often associated with sickness, pain and suffering and often leaves a great void. But for the Christian it is gain (Phil. 1:21).

When death comes we will either be prepared or unprepared. We can experience either the joys or the horrors that await. We can be escorted by angels or awaken to torments. The choice is ours; the choice is present. The choice is life; the choice is death. I have chosen life.

Testimony

The time was dismal and everyone knew the end was near. There they stood, at the bedside of Augusta Ellen Harris. Weak, frail and with her body failing, she looked up with enthusiastic hope. "Do you see those angels?" she asked, and then she passed into eternity. That is the testimony of a grandmother who had trusted Christ as Lord and Savior. It was sincere; it was biblical. We read of Lazarus, who died and was carried by the angels to the arms of a loving, compassionate Father. However, alongside the death of Lazarus we read of a man who died having trusted in his self-sufficiency. He was not carried by the angels, but was buried. In hell, he "lifted up his eyes, being in torments" (Lk. 16:23).

Friend, make preparations for eternal life. I beg you to prepare for death before it comes. As stated at the beginning of this book, death cannot be bought, bribed or defeated. You can't outrun it or outsmart it. The only way around the fate of death is Jesus. Ω

To Walk Alive:
Salvation Made Plain

1. Realize your situation (Rom. 3:10).
2. Know that all are sinners (Rom. 3:23).
3. Find the reason all are sinners (Rom. 5:12).
4. See the result of being a sinner (Rom. 6:23).
5. Know God's concern for sinners (Rom. 5:8).
6. Follow God's way of salvation (Rom. 10:9,10,13).
7. Find a Bible-believing church (Heb. 10:25).
8. Be baptized (Acts 2:41).
9. Continue to follow Jesus (Matt. 16:24).

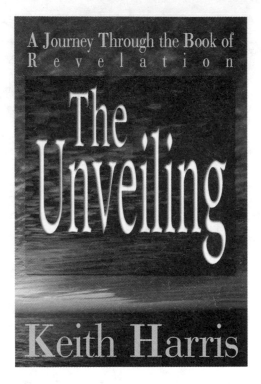

The Unveiling

The Unveiling is a verse by verse study of the book of
Revelation. The book of Revelation is greater than any
mystery novel or suspense thriller. *The Unveiling* supplies
answers to many perplexing questions of life: What happens
after death? Is the Earth going to be our eternal dwelling?
Who will be at the Great White Throne Judgment? What
comes after the Millennium? *The Unveiling* probes areas of
Revelation not normally ventured by today's theologians,
making it a most enlightening and adventurous journey
pertaining to life and the complexities of the afterlife. Fully
outlined, indexed, cross-referenced and charted for easy
access to any given aspect of Revelation.
490 pages -$16.99